The Case Study

A Business Novel

How To

Start, Run, and Sell a Business

By: Randal Roberts

Preface

This is not an all-encompassing text book on the various aspects of starting, running, and selling a business, but more of an overview, a case study, if you will, to give the reader a holistic look at some of the hurdles and struggles that may arise along the way. There are hundreds of books written that touch on each and every concept that will be discussed. If you desire a more in-depth discussion about certain topics and concepts you will be able to find many that will suit your needs.

Also, there are several issues with each different industry and every business related to that industry, therefore, some things may not pertain to your situation, but most concepts should relate to your circumstances. Starting a business will be exciting, rewarding, frustrating, taxing, worrisome, exhausting, and most any other feeling that you can imagine. Put on your seatbelt and hold on tight, because it will not be a smooth journey.

I wish you success, but you must have perseverance in your endeavor. It is not for the soft-hearted person, or someone who is not willing to put forth the correct effort and show real grit. Good luck for a happy landing.

The Case Study Begins

An Introduction

It was early in the morning, before the dogs were even awake. Dan and I decided to walk the nine-hole executive course before we hit our respective offices. We figured that walking and carrying our clubs would give us a little exercise.

Dan was off trying to find an errant tee shot, and I was walking straight down the fairway, carrying my bag of clubs slung over my shoulder, walking in rhythm to the sound of my clubs swaying back and forth. As I walked, the clubs kept making a muffled clanging sound, hitting each other as I moved forward.

The Golf Club where we played had an eighteen-hole championship course and a small nine-hole executive version. Both courses were good and each served its purpose. The eighteen-hole course was always very busy, but the niner was more sporadic. That made it easy just to show up and play. They were both wonderful attractions featuring sprawling, well-manicured lawns, unpredictable waves of rolling hills, trees, tall grasses along the edge of the fairways that lead to erratically shaped sand bunkers. The greens were in excellent condition, and the ball rolled without the slightest hint of a bump. The courses were in superb condition.

It was early in the fall and I was wearing a windbreaker to keep off the early morning chill. What a beautiful day it was shaping up to be.

"What a great idea to come down this morning," I said to Dan, as we teed off on the next hole.

No one else was playing on the course, but in the distance we could hear a mower or two. One was on a green that I could see across the small valley and the other mower was rolling up and down a long par five.

"That's what I want to do when I get too old to work at a real job," I thought to myself. "Just think of the peace. No phone calls. No boss watching my every move. Not even office chatter. What a respite that would

5

offer." I wanted it sooner than later but did not know how to make it happen. So I just changed the subject of my mind back to golf.

Dan was not much of a talker. He talked, but no idle babble. When he said anything, I took note. He had been through a lot and had a lot to teach. In fact, I played golf with him just to pick up some nuggets of wisdom, as many as I could anyway.

After a few holes, the sun began to peek out from the top of the mountain on the east side of the valley. Looking at the mountainside, you could already see some color since the trees had begun to change. What a delight! Golfing just a few miles from majestic mountains in the early morning, with the course all to ourselves! I felt like a rich man.

As we played, I kept thinking about the idea of not having a boss or phone calls and all the other stuff that goes with a job. Dan seemed to have it made. He worked when he wanted, or if he wanted. He had been a commercial banker for many years, then one day he started his own company. He seemed to have done very well. All he did now was manage his investments and whatever else he chose, like golf. I thought it seemed like a good life. One that I could get used to.

At the next tee box I asked, "So, how did you do it?"

"Do what?" he asked.

"You know, start your own business and make it successful," I responded.

"Oh, come on now. You don't want to go through what I did. You really don't want to start your own business. It's too hard, I'm telling you," he said with a bit of disgust in his voice, trying to persuade me to not even go there.

"No, really," I responded in a serious tone. "I think I could do it. You know, start and run my own business."

"Do you realize that somewhere between fifty and ninety percent of all start-ups fail in the first five years?" he asked. "The percentage depends on where the info came from and who is running the Small Business Administration. Either way, it is a high percentage of failure."

"Why do you think it is so high?" I questioned.

"I've got to tee off. Just leave it for now, please," he responded as he lined up his shot.

He did not hit that shot too well. I must have shaken him with my questions.

'Sorry if I distracted you with my question," I said apologetically.

"Don't worry about it. I'm just not on my game today," Dan said.

As we walked down the fairway in silence, with only the sound of the clubs in our bags, I kept thinking about starting my own business. But what kind of business would it be? How could I figure it out? I had some good business experience and figured I was as smart as anyone. Maybe smarter, I don't know.

"It would be cool to be my own boss and not answer to anyone. Yes, I could do that," I thought with a little conviction. "Thousands of others have done it. Why not me? Yes, why not me?" I said, continuing to mumble to myself.

Right then, I determined that my new goal in life was to start and run my own business. First, I would have to figure out what, how, when, etc. There was a lot to think about, and my mind went into high gear.

We had just finished the round and as we walked to the parking lot, I asked Dan, "Well, will you give me all of the things I need to learn to start one up?"

"Start one what?" he asked.

"My new business," I responded.

"Are you still on that idea?" he questioned.

"Yes, sir," I said. "Will you help me?"

His countenance began to change slightly and he showed a little puzzle in his look.

"On one condition," he stated after a pause.

"Name it," I said enthusiastically.

"I will do it, but only on the golf course. No office, no homework for me. Just talk," he ordered.

"Deal. I'm going to count on you," I yelled over the parked cars.

"OK. Deal," he responded a bit reluctantly.

I don't think he thought I would really follow up on my request.

"See ya next time," I said.

He just nodded and said, "Adios." And gave a little menacing smile as he climbed in behind the wheel.

START OR BUY
YOUR BUSINESS

1

Questions

Dan Griffin and I met at a company event a few years back. He was the banker for the company I worked for, so he attended the gathering. He was a few years older than me, but we hit it off from the get-go and had done a few things together, like golf and biking. We even jogged together a few times.

My wife Lori worked as a marketing professional at a local advertising firm. She did not have much financial knowledge but was good with the people side of things. She had a clear way of thinking that complemented my narrow financial mind. We were a good match there, I thought.

Our wives were the ones who really jelled. They became good friends and went to lunch several times a month. Many of our meetings were at races they participated in. They both helped a local charity, and running races was their specialty. They helped set the races up and did a lot of volunteer work and even ran in a few. Dan and I participated in some of the 10K's they sponsored. It was fun times.

My specialty was accounting and finance. Mostly arranging and managing loans for the few companies I worked for. It gave me a working knowledge of how to read and apply financial information in a business.

That said, I really didn't know how to begin or even what to work toward.

That evening at dinner, my wife and I discussed it. She wasn't totally against it but seemed to be a little perplexed at why I wanted to try it because I had a good job and the money was fine.

"Well," she said, "I know of a few reasons why you shouldn't consider starting your own business."

"Yeh, what are they?" I asked.

"Don't do it because you hate your boss or just because you have been doing the same thing for so long."

"That make sense," I commented. "What else?"

"How about a few things like, you don't want to wake up early or you want to set your own hours or even you want to get rich. Those are not really valid reasons because you will probably have longer hours and customers telling you what to do," she spouted. "You might even make less money for a few years, too. Maybe even forever."

"Is that it?" I asked with a bit of a snicker in my voice.

"I guess there are a million reason why not to start a business," she concluded.

"Well, if you are so smart, give me a few valid reasons why to do this."

"Well maybe you have a good innovative idea or maybe you can do something better than anyone else. Those are valid," she said. "I think if someone has a passion or natural talent in a certain area, those are good reasons also. Here again, there will be many good reasons to start your own business. I can't name them all for you."

"That is good advice. Any other suggestions for me?" I asked more humbly.

"No, I don't think so. I do think you need to spend a lot of time thinking about how you want to spend your days and weeks and months, if this is really for you, for me, for us. Most of all, does it make sense?"

"Wow, there is a lot to think about, isn't there? I had better give it some time to sink in and spend a lot of time exploring all of the options," I stated.

"Good idea," she responded. "We do need a roof over our heads and food on the table. I am sort of used to those things. I really don't think we can live on my salary alone."

"I understand those concerns too. Thanks for the input," I said, putting a fork full of meat in my mouth. Just as I did, I remembered reading an article earlier in the week.

"Well, I was reading something the other day about why a successful entrepreneur, the author of the article, began his business. The article said something like this: There are basically two core reasons to start a business. One is to make a good living for yourself and the other reason is to create an asset that can be exchanged for loads of money down the road. A nest egg, if you will. Those two are the lowest common denominators is what the guy was saying in the article," I told her as she listened intently. "He went on to say that if you start a business, it needs to be something that someone else is willing to buy. Don't create a business that no one wants. If you do it becomes an anchor around your neck. I don't need any anchors around my neck."

"Amen to that," she responded. "But what if you just have this idea that you cannot get out of your head? Maybe it is an innovative whatever, but just something that nags your brain? Money can't be one of the top motivators to begin a business. Can it?"

"I guess not, I think, but most of those kinds of ideas usually turn into a hobby or a side thing," I answered.

"Nice ideas, but my show is coming on and I just want to veg out this evening," she said, as she settled in to her favorite spot on the couch.

Concept #1

Think long and hard about what, where, why, how and when to start a business.

2

Family

I really did not want my boss or any of my coworkers to know I had become serious with this idea, so I asked a few hypothetical questions to some fellow workers, just to get their take on the subject. I was really surprised to know that several of them had some of the same thoughts. As I thought about it, I felt that it is really the American dream: to own your own business, become productive in order to help others improve their lives, contribute your share, and provide a good living for your family. Those, I thought, were good reasons to move forward.

After a few weeks of asking questions around the office and to anyone else who would listen, I was surprised at how many had thought of both apprehensions and constructive ideas that had not even crossed my mind. Things like having family members in the business and what that could do to the relationships that had been developed in those families. One guy gave this example: "My grandfather was one of seven children. Several of the boys began to build cars from old parts they found around the neighborhood or parts they could beg from various places. They made a little money and the business turned into a full time auto repair service. As success grew and as the money grew, the next generation wanted to be a part of the business. The problem was that not all family members had the right skills or temperament to work in the business, but they all felt entitled to be there. The thing turned into a mess, which caused the business to split and no one ever was able to match the success that the original shop generated."

"It doesn't sound like the family did too well in the long run," I commented.

"Well, I am the third generation and most of my cousins are able to gather a few times each year. I can't say as much for my dad and his siblings," he confessed. "It has been a struggle most of my life to watch the unrest there has been."

"I don't want that to happen in my family," I thought. "We get along pretty well, so far."

"This can't happen to every family, can it?" I asked another colleague who was part of our conversation.

"I have heard of some horror stories as well, but I have also heard of a few good ones, too," he added.

"Well, I need to hear one, if you can remember the details," I said.

"The way I heard it went sort of like this. It was not my family but one of my friends that I grew up with. One of the sisters in the family thought up an idea for a small part to fit on strollers to help mothers better use their baby strollers. It was an attachment that gave the mom the ability to hold cups or bottles and things like that. At the time, most strollers were just that, strollers. Nothing fancy, just a means to push a baby around a park or a store or wherever. One of her brothers had a mechanical mind and built a prototype. Her sister had several business law classes in college and began the process to obtain a patent. Another brother was a salesman and began to contact stroller manufactures and after-market retailers to sell the parts. The brother who was mechanical found a facility to make the parts. Everyone had his own little niche where they excelled. The woman who invented the part, became the champion for the product and customers service department. Their mother was an accountant and kept the books while their father sort of bankrolled the thing until it got off the ground. It was really a match made in heaven."

"What happened?" I asked with a little excitement in my voice.

"Over time, they built up the business, opened their own little manufacturing shop, and kept going. About ten years into it, they were bought out by a larger company and the family had enough to invest in some real estate properties and wound up not having to work as hard. I sort of lost track of them when I moved here to take this job," he concluded.

"Now that is how I want things to end," I said with too much enthusiasm in my voice.

That evening Lori and I discussed the happy ending story at dinner. She liked that outcome, too. Her family had too much going on already and did not need to take on any more challenges. Mine wasn't much better.

"Well, I can just start a business and then find good workers and not worry about family," I said to her.

"Then, you have to worry about employees and taxes and all the rest," she stated.

"That's sure true. I will worry about all that later," I told her.

"So one more thing," Lori stated. "What happens when you are tired of the whole thing and you want to retire, if that is ever an option for you?"

"Good question. I asked one of the guys, in the conversation I told you about, that very question."

"Well, what did he tell you?" she asked.

"He told me that it is important to have an exit plan at the very beginning of the whole process. The plan can change over time, but there needs to be some kind of plan," I repeated to her.

"What do you mean by the term *exit plan*?" she asked with a confused look on her face.

"Basically, it is a pre-determination of how you will get rid of the business when the time is right. I did some reading about this subject on the internet, and it was pretty interesting. You either determine to sell it, close it down, or hand it off to your children. There is more to it than that, but it gets a little complicated, and I am getting tired. So, maybe later," I said, trying to end the discussion.

"Well, don't leave me hanging. Give me at least a quick primer," she requested.

"Ok. Here is the *Reader's Digest* version. When you want to retire or do something different and don't want to be saddled with a business, you need to give it, sell it, or close it down, but you have to think about the employees, your tax consequences, and all the assets that are part of the business. It takes lawyers and CPAs to help figure out the best way to unload the thing," I told her.

"I guess you could file bankruptcy and just shut the doors, but that is a different discussion. Besides if it is a good business that would not even be a consideration," I concluded.

"Well, I hope you can either sell it and take me on a trip around the world or give it to our children, if we ever find out how we get some of those things," she said with a smirk on her face.

Concept #2

Be very careful not to destroy family ties along the way.

(Not all family members are suited to be part of your business,

and exit planning is a must in the beginning.)

3

Emotional Check

A few weeks later, maybe even a month or more, Dan and I were at the links again. My game had not improved much, but neither had his. We were both just a couple of hackers thinking we were real golfers. I never would be either, but I did believe I could be an owner of my own business.

After having many conversations with my wife, friends and co-workers, it seemed like most of them had the same dream, but none of them had ever tried to move in that direction. It was as if they gave up even before they started. I guess I had been that way for many years, but not now. I was determined to make it happen. Exactly what "it" was I didn't know yet, but I was farther down the road than I was the last time I played golf.

"Wow, look at that one. It is your best drive of the day," I congratulated Dan. "I don't think you could hit one straighter than that. It got a good bounce and great roll. Nice job."

All he said was, "Thanks. Now let's go see how far it actually went." We headed down the fairway.

"I figure it's got to be at least two hundred and seventy-five yards. It out flew mine," I commented.

"Yes. That did turn out nicely didn't it?" he said.

On my second shot, I shanked one, then another, and then flew the green on my approach shot. Finally, after hitting the green it took me three putts to get it in the hole.

"That is maddening and frustrating, I get so angry when I do that," I blurted out.

"Now, now, now. We need to keep calm. You know running you own business can be like that," he commented.

I looked up in surprise and asked, "What do you mean?"

"Oh, when you are running your own business, you will have great days and not so great days. Just like golf. Sometimes you hit them good and sometimes you couldn't hit the side of a barn," Dan pontificated.

Well, I didn't know for myself, but I could imagine. It gave me a nice opening into something that had been on my mind as I went about interviewing everyone I knew.

"Did you ever have bad days when you started?" I asked.

"I had bad days when I started, in the middle and throughout, even until I sold the thing. Then for months after selling, it I questioned myself. Did I get enough for it? Will he run it like I did? Will my old clients be happy? All those things go through your mind, and it can make you crazy if you let it. That is part of the reason I took up golf. To clear my mind and focus on things other than the business and my mistakes, fears, and concerns," he told me as his tone faded off toward the end, as if some of the memories were flooding back into his mind.

"It must have been hard," I said.

"Harder than you can imagine. Harder than golf, I think." Dan commented. "Playing golf is not your livelihood and in the long run doesn't affect anyone else except maybe one's ego. Of course, it would be a lot different if you were a pro golfer, but you are not. Business does matter to many people. People like your family, employees and their families, suppliers, and customers. They can all be positively or negatively affected. You win, most of them win. But if you lose, most will lose along with you. It can be serious."

"It sort of sounds scary," I responded. "Is it a total burden all the time?"

"Not at all. There are many times, good times, all along the way. It can give you an opportunity to help many people in so many different ways. Think about for a second. You are creating jobs, paying taxes, and helping whoever uses your products or services. It can be very rewarding. And it is, most of the time, but not always. It can make your emotions go up and down, and some people can't handle those kinds of emotional swings," he preached.

"Nice putt. Where did you find that one?" Dan asked.

"It was much better than the last hole. I guess it is like running a business," I commented with a bit of a chuckle.

"Just keep that in mind, if and when you decide to take the leap," he told me.

"Good advice," I thought to myself.

Driving home, I began to think about what Dan had told me regarding the emotions and all. "What if I started a business and it didn't make it? How would we survive? What would I do then? How could I pay back whoever I owed money to? Those and many similar questions flooded into my mind. It was almost overwhelming. I felt a heaviness press down on my body, as if someone laid a big heavily weighted blanket over my shoulders. I shook my head and said to myself, "Snap out of it! It is just in your mind. Nothing has happened yet. You still have a job. Take a chill pill."

This is what went through my mind on my drive home. I decided then to find ways to keep my emotions in check, such as playing golf or going for a long walk, if problems began to arise. "Yes, that is what I would do, take long walks on a golf course to keep on an even keel. Great idea!" I thought as I drove.

Concept #3

Running your own business may be very trying on your emotions and the emotions of those around you.

4

What is the Plan?

After the nightmarish drive home, I arrived just in time to meet Lori at the back door.

"Where are you going?" I asked.

"You didn't answer your phone so I'm on my way to pick up Chinese for dinner. I phoned in an order and was hoping to catch you. But no! You should keep your phone on," she scolded.

I pulled the phone out of my pocket and sure enough, a missed call from Lori.

"I'm sorry. Hey, let's ride together," I suggested. "We can eat there. The food will be hotter."

"Good idea," she responded with a little bit better tone in her voice.

As we climbed into the car, Lori asked, "What is bugging you? You are usually good at answering the phone, driving or not."

"Oh, it was my discussion with Dan at the golf course," I told her.

"Well, it must have been serious for you to be so absent minded," she remarked.

"Dan was telling me about some of the emotional ups and downs with running your own business. Some of it sounded frightening," I began.

"You can tell me all about it over a plate of Moo Goo Gai Pan," she urged.

"Uh, is that what she ordered? Not my favorite," I thought silently.

We arrived at the restaurant and walked in. The owner knew us well and seated us in our usual spot as the waiter came over.

"I have a phone order for you, Ms. Lori," he said with a puzzled look on his face.

"We decided to come inside and have our meal here. Can you plate if for us?" she asked pleasantly.

"Sure. No problem," he responded.

"Uh, Charlie. Can you get me some dumplings and two egg rolls to go along with that order?" I asked as Lori stole a look at me. I am sure she was wondering why.

"Sure. No problem, Charlie," he responded. We called each other Charlie. It was a thing we had going.

"Thank you," I told him.

"So what was so important that you didn't answer your phone earlier?" Lori questioned.

As the waiter brought out the egg drop soup for Lori and the egg rolls and dumplings for me, I responded, "We discussed the emotional side of owning a business."

"And?" she said with an inquisitive look on her face.

With the light on her face and reflecting from her jet black hair, I remembered why I wanted to marry her. She was really stunning. After living with someone for a while you tend to forget some of the why in a relationship. I hoped I would never forget.

"Why are you looking at me like that?" she asked.

"That is exactly what we talked about today," I told her.

"About me?" she asked with a real questioning look.

"Well, about you and our family, friends and, well, just about everyone we know," I said.

"What were you drinking?" she asked in a playful voice.

"Nothing. It was just the seriousness of leaving a full time position, working for someone else, and then going out on your own. There are a lot of people who can learn to be dependent on you when you own a business.

Do you understand what I am saying?" I asked her. She still had a puzzled look on her face.

"Go on. I can't wait to hear what's next," she urged.

"If I quit my job and start a business, then hire people to help me and get customers and use various suppliers, in a way all of these people become somewhat dependent on me. It is a lot of responsibility, you know," I said seriously.

"OK, I sort of see where you are coming from on this," Lori responded. "Go on."

"If the business should fail, what about all those people and their children and their homes and college tuition and their bills and on and on. If I fail, they fail. We all fail and then how do they and we survive? If I do this, I need some plan to implement in case of this kind of emergency. It only seems right," I said.

"No wonder you didn't answer your phone. Those are frightening thoughts," Lori concluded.

"Exactly my point. There really needs to be some kind of plan in place just in case the worse happens. I will need to figure that one out before I even get started," I said almost to myself as Charlie showed up with a couple of plates of hot food.

"I am glad I filled up on the egg rolls and dumplings," I thought to myself.

"What kind of plan would that be?" she asked.

"I don't really know, but bankruptcy is one way. I think they call it Chapter 11, or something like that. I will need to get some legal advice about it." I said. "I really think that bankruptcy would be a last-ditch answer to business financial difficulties. It could leave a lot of people holding the bag for my mistakes. I don't really like that idea."

"No, that does not sound good. I don't like it either," she said with resilience.

"I am guessing that before a business ever gets to that point, the owner would get investors or borrow money or try to sell the thing. A small loss would be better than a large one and also stiffing creditors and maybe employees." I reassured myself. "Yes, that is it. Try to sell it, even for a lower price, unless I could come up with a plan that would win over existing or new investors. Those would be better alternatives. One more alternative would be to take on a partner, but it would not work in my case," I suggested.

"What do you mean?" Lori asked.

"Well, if I were to have a partner and things went poorly or one of the partners were to become incapacitated, you know, not able to work and contribute because of death or injury, some kind of 'buy-sell' agreement would be appropriate." I told her, wearing on her patience just a little.

"What does that even mean?" she questioned.

"It is sort of like a marriage prenuptial agreement, but for business partners. If one partner wants out, for whatever reason, the agreement spells out exactly what and how things will be handled. Things like, who pays who and how much. And, who gets what after a settlement. That way each partner is covered from the outset, before the business even gets going. A pretty smart idea, I think. How about you?" I asked Lori, as she was yawning.

"Maybe we should have had one of those, that determined how long I had to listen to you ramble. Just kidding, dear. I really need to get back to the house. I have a project to finish up before bed time," she told me.

"Ok, all right. Let's go. One more thing, though. Part of this agreement, or in a separate agreement, there should be some sort of succession plan. You know, if something was to happen. It could spell out how the business is able to keep operating. That's it. Let's go," I said as Charlie brought the check.

"You were good as usual," I told him.

"Thanks for coming in, Charlie. Have a nice evening," he said with a smile and a wave of the hand.

I was still in a funk but managed to give him a smile and a wave of my hand.

"Thank you, sir," I told him as we left.

Concept #4

You need to have a plan if things go wrong and the business fails.

5

Start or Buy

It was my day to play golf with Dan, but the weather was not cooperating. My wipers were going as fast I they could but didn't even come close to keeping the rain off the windshield. When I left home it was just cloudy, but about halfway to the course the heavens opened up and let it all out. Wow, what a storm. I didn't want to walk from the parking lot, so I pulled into the clubhouse and let the valet park my car.

"Thanks man. I really appreciate your being here," I told the kid as I handed him some money.

"No problem. I'm already wet and the tips are great today. I think Dan is inside waiting for you," he said as he closed the door to drive off.

I walked in the Grille, and Dan was at a seat that overlooked the eighteenth green. It was his favorite spot in the bistro.

"I guess it is a rainout today," I said, walking up to the table.

"I'm sure you're right," he agreed.

"Want some lunch? I'm buying," I blurted out.

"You buy? Now that will be a treat," he responded. "I think you owe me anyway from our last match."

As I sat down, Dan motioned to the waiter for a couple of drinks.

"Well, I hope you have some interesting news to talk about, because I'm not driving in this mess. I will wait it out right here," he said in an assured tone. "Besides, this is my favorite spot to sit. It offers great views."

"Oh, I have plenty to talk about, but it is not local or national news," I responded.

"Well, what could it be?" he asked as the waiter came to the table with our drinks.

He took our order, but we told him to hold it back for fifteen or twenty minutes while we talked.

"You know I am really intent on having my own business. I don't know what it will be yet, although I have my eye on a few options," I began.

"Before you tell me your secrets, I have a thing or two I have been mulling over since last week," Dan said, as he cut me off.

"Well, I'm all ears, sir," I responded.

"There are really only three or four ways to get into business."

"OK. That is a good place to start," I encouraged him on. "Tell me what they are."

"Really three viable alternatives for you, but four for some others," he proceeded. "The one that will not fit you is that you cannot inherit a business because you have no one to inherit it from. So that one does not count in this case."

"Tell me the three that do count," I sort of begged.

"Here are your options. One, you can start a business from scratch; from the ground up. No customers, no anything. Two, you can buy an existing business, one that is a going concern, and the owner is just ready to sell and go golfing. Number three, is you can buy a franchise, where the how-to's and must haves are mostly done for you," he concluded.

"That makes sense for me, but how does one decide?" I asked. "Is there any magic formula to it?"

"Let me explain each in a little more detail and then your question should be answered," he responded.

"Number one. Start a business from scratch. This seems to be the hardest to make happen. This is usually done by people who have a special skill or a super idea. For example, a restaurateur, someone who has a talent to make a certain type of food. It also could be a craftsman, a person who has a special talent in a chosen field like plumbing or some other trade. Many of these businesses start out as hobbies or by someone who works for a similar business, but believes they can do a better job on their own. These kinds of businesses are hard to get outside financing to start up. The money usually comes from savings or family and friends. One major problem with a complete start-up is that the entrepreneur is usually one-dimensional. They know the trade but do not necessarily know how to run a business on their own."

Dan wanted to keep going, but I interrupted him, "This does not sound like me. I know finance but have no real trade nor do I have any special skills, in all honesty," I commented.

"That is a valid observation and something that needs to be considered with care and thought," he added.

"I think I get your point here. What about the other two?" I urged him on.

"Give me time. I will get there," he quipped.

"Just to finish up number one. You may know your trade, but can you attract customers or keep the accounting records or even make a plan of all the odd tasks that need to be done? Maybe they do not know how to sell themselves or their product or service. Or maybe it is the bookkeeping or supply chain management. You know, those kinds of things can be hard for many. These are just a few of the questions and things to think about before you try to go it from scratch," he said, as he finished the first option.

"And number two?" I asked in eager anticipation.

"Number two just might be where you will want to go," he began.

"Buy a business that is already up and running. It sounds easy, but just wait until I explain to you all that could be involved," he went on.

"Well, don't scare me yet," I responded.

"There could be hundreds of things to look at in buying a business, depending on what kind it is and how large, etc. There are companies and consultants who spend their whole business lives finding, buying, and selling businesses. It can range from the simple to the extremely complex transaction. Here are just a few of the things you should consider. You may want to hire a business broker to help you, but at least read a book that goes into all the detail. Most small businesses will be listed with a business broker, but they represent the seller. You may want to hire a different broker or advisor or consultant to help you with your side of the contract."

"OK, that makes sense. But what are the hundreds of things to look at that you mentioned?" I asked.

"To understand them all, like I said, buy a good book that goes into detail or find it all on the internet. But I will outline some of the more important items. They can vary from industry to industry."

By this time our food had arrived, and we began to make some small talk about the latest event that our wives were involved in. It was a 5K walk/run for one of the causes their local charity was working on. It was a good cause, but I was not interested in a 5k walk/run. Dan did not seem too interested either. I am sure the ladies would get us to spend a few hours helping them in some way. That was a given.

I placed the first bite of food in my mouth and could smell the fresh cooked beef when a huge clap of thunder sounded. It startled me to the point that I missed my mouth.

"Uh, that looks good on your shirt," Dan joked. "It adds color to your outfit. That looks like the shot you had on seven last week. Nice miss."

"Wow! That was a loud one." We both laughed at my miss, or should I say mess?

We ate without speaking for a few minutes as we listened to the thunder and watched the lightning flash outside. The rain was still coming down in sheets. The course would be too wet the rest of the day, even if it stopped raining right now.

"So much for golf today," I stated.

"That is the most correct thing I've heard you say the whole day." Dan must have been in a playful mood.

"How's the food?" I asked.

"Free food is always good to me. Thanks for the treat," he quipped again. "Let's get back to our conversation. I think we were at number two."

"Right, number two," I echoed.

"Number two is to buy an existing business. I told you a few minutes ago that there could be hundreds of things to look at, to ask questions about, or to investigate. It can range from fairly simple to extremely complicated. If I were your business advisor I would begin with a list of questions to ask after I took a look at the most recent set of financial information, including, but not limited to, a balance sheet, income statement, and cash flow statement. I would also obtain the prior three fiscal year end information and tax returns."

"Well, fortunately I understand financial information, but if I did not have my current experience how could I find out what to look at and look for?" I asked.

"Again, books and the internet are where you could go. Also, a business broker or trusted advisor would come in handy to help along the way. It may cost some money up front, but in the long run someone like that could more than pay for himself," he reinforced.

"OK, I got it. Research the heck out of it until I figure it out. Right?" I responded.

"Correct. I think you understand, finally," he chided.

"I will give you a list of questions that you will need to ask. Remember, one more time, it depends on the kind, size, and age of the business. There are many different aspects to all kinds of different businesses. These questions are not in any order, but once you find a good business to buy, you will understand what order to ask them in. You will probably be required to sign a non-disclosure/non-compete document in order to look at the records. Private companies are called private for certain reasons."

He went on, "You know that a list of questions will be forgotten unless written, so why don't you make a list of questions, and I will take a look at them to see if you missed anything."

"Oh, that is a great idea. I appreciate the suggestion," I responded.

"Hey, the sun is beginning to peek out from behind that cloud over there," Dan said, pointing his finger toward a few rays of sunshine.

"That's great. I really need to get going. Thanks for the time and info today," I said.

"Thanks for the lunch. You'll have to do it again for me. I love free lunches," Dan said as we walked toward the door.

"That was the cheapest advice I had gotten in a long time. Lunch for all that info, a steal," I thought.

As we walked out toward the front, it hit me. "Hey, we never talked about option number three," I commented.

"I didn't bring it up because I figured you were sold on option number two. It won't take too long if you want to hang here for a few more minutes," he offered.

"Let's do it now, so I can think through them all tonight and over the next few days," I responded.

"OK, have a seat right there, and we can finish up," he instructed, pointing to a couple of chairs in the foyer of the club. "Number three is to buy a franchise of some kind, but there are pluses and minuses involved when buying a franchise."

"Can we go through the top three or four of each?" I requested.

"Sure. The pluses are that the product if virtually prepacked, along with the marketing, operating side, equipment, if needed, and the store design. It is a package-deal, no real creative juices need to be used."

"Well, that sure sounds good," I said quickly.

"Then consider the downside. It is expensive to get into, you have to buy goods and marketing from the franchisor, and you pretty much have to do things their way, with no variance. It can be onerous, if I can use that word," Dan told me. "Advertising alone can cost thousands and can be a hard number to make."

"Are there a large number of franchises to pick from?" I asked.

"There are only a few thousand or so. Most stores you see around are franchise stores, from restaurants, to vehicle maintenance shops. You name it, and it is probably franchised," Dan told me. "Some can cost up to millions to open and once you open a location you are saddled to the building rent and the equipment and the employee training and managing and all the rest. Then to top it off, you generally have to pay about eight percent of your sales as a franchise fee. And that is forever. This does not include ongoing purchases of supplies and inventory. So you see why I used the work onerous."

After a pause, he went on, "I am not slamming franchises, but it is important to thoroughly investigate all aspects of a deal before you sign your name on the dotted line. There are a lot of people making very good money with franchises. Some will even buy the rights for a certain territory, either a city or a whole state. So, it is not a total no-go, but it is not for everyone. A franchise is a good route for someone who wants to manage a business but who does not have any new ideas or special learned skills."

"Wow. That is a lot to think about. I will do a bit of research on franchises as I contemplate the other two options as well. Thanks again for your time. I hope the weather will be better next week," I told him.

We gave our valet tickets to the kid at the door, who hustled off to grab the car.

"Whose will he get first?" I asked.

"Did you give him more than a ten dollar tip?" Dan asked.

"I gave him five, thinking I would have to give him another five when I left," I told him.

"He will bring my car first," Dan said with confidence.

Sure enough, into the portico came Dan's car.

"You win again," I told him.

"I'll send you the email with the list of questions. Thanks again for lunch," he said. He ducked his head to get in the driver's seat.

"I'll look for that email, and thanks. I am sure the weather will hold up next week," I said.

Dan waved as he pulled away. My car showed up, and I gave the kid another five. It had stopped raining. I was cheap, so that is all he got from me.

Concept #5

Decide how to begin your business.

(Start from scratch, buy an existing business, or buy a franchise?)

6

Legal Structure

Later that evening, I was looking around the internet and came across some interesting things. One thing that stuck out to me was that I needed to pick a legal structure for my new business. How was I to know which to pick. Did it have to do with bookkeeping or taxes or some laws? I really didn't know, so I decided to call my old school buddy, Wally.

Wallace Jacobson was his real name and the name he used on his stationery. I guess he figured it sounded more proper. Wally was fair haired and about six foot two in height. He was a likeable guy and was married to his high school sweetheart, Helen. They were a great couple.

Anyway, he had been in practice for a number of years doing things like small business litigation, wills, trusts, and that sort of thing. He was in a private practice and had never been with a big firm. Wally was down to earth. I could relate to him, so I made the call.

"Hey Wally, it's Ross, how you doing?" I asked as he answered his own phone.

"Well, no wonder it rained today. You haven't called in a while. Are you in trouble, again?" he asked.

"What do you mean, again?" I asked.

After some of the normal small talk, we got down to business.

"What can I do for you?" Wally asked.

"I got this wild hair about opening my own business and just had a few questions for you," I responded.

"I guess I better turn off the clock," he quipped.

"If this goes through, you will get plenty of billings from me, so don't worry," I assured him. "I am just wondering what kind of legal entity would be the best to start a new business."

He gave out a bit of a sigh and said, "That could be a big answer or a small one. I don't have time right now for the big one, so let me give you just a few things to think about. It seems to me is that where you are, for right now."

"Yes, the short version is the one I need tonight. I am just doing a lot of research and trying to put my ideas and thoughts together," I told him. "Hit it."

"To begin with, there are a few basic types of business entities, which progress from a sole proprietorship or partnership to a Limited Liability Company (LLC), then an S Corporation (S Corp) and finally to a full-fledged C Corporation (C Corp). There can be varying other types, but these are the major kinds of entities. Let me go into a little more detail, but I recommend that you look up the definitions in the *Investopedia* on the internet or in any kind of financial/legal dictionary. It will give a more detailed explanation. A sole proprietorship is the most simple. It really takes no legal filings to speak of and only comes in to play when tax time arrives. This means that you file taxes as an individual using what is called a Schedule C on your tax return. All income and expenses are taxed to the proprietor, the owner," he explained.

"Yes, I am aware of this form of entity. My mother did this when she opened a little boutique that lasted less than one year," I said perceptively.

"The problem is that any and all liability becomes and stays as personal liability. If someone gets hurt on the job or on your business premises, you can be personally liable for whatever happens. It can be scary. If the company does not make it and has to close, then all the liabilities become personal liabilities and must be paid by you, the owner. Some very small operators use this because it is quick and easy and usually they do things on their own. It can work in some cases. But I do not recommend this type of entity for you," he advised.

"Next, we have a partnership. There a number of different kinds of partnerships, but they work very much like a proprietorship except you are in business with one or more other individuals. I won't go into this one because it seems like you want to do this alone."

I responded, "That's correct. I want to do this thing all by myself."

"That is what I thought," he said.

"Next, let's go into a LLC. This is similar to a sole proprietorship except the liability is transferred to the legal entity. The taxes work pretty much the same, but there is one thin layer of protection against unforeseen liability. Many new businesses begin with this kind of organization. It takes an application to the IRS and to the state to get the name registered and reserved. You will, sooner or later, need to visit with an accountant, preferably a Certified Public Accountant (CPA) to go through all of the tax ramifications that are involved with each type of entity that I am telling you about," Wally strongly advised. "It is very, very important to do this."

"The next step up, if I can say it that way, is an S Corp. This adds one extra thin layer of liability protection, but complicates the taxes just a little. Here again, a good CPA will be worth the money invested. Remember, you may only get one chance to create a business on your own. So do it right the first time and save headaches down the road."

"Good advice," I thought to myself.

"The final form of entity that I want to explain to you is the C Corp. This divorces you from the liability as much as possible, but it adds a lot more tax headaches and requires a separate tax filing for the business as a stand-alone entity. It gives the owner or owners as much protection as there possibly can be. Anyone can take anyone else to court for whatever or whenever, if they have enough money to pay guys like me. A C Corp will require additional filings in most states, so there is more paperwork to do. I think most states allow the paperwork to be done online. That seems much easier. One last thing is that most professional investors want to invest in this type of a structure," he finished.

"Wow, I obviously have not thought through all the details required in starting a business. It can be mind boggling, to say the least," I said in bewilderment.

"Wally, I really appreciate your time and when I get this thing going will you be my legal eyes and ears?" I asked him.

"I will be proud to represent you, as long as you promise to keep your nose as clean as possible," he responded.

"I promise," I said as we said our good byes.

"Say 'hi' to Helen for me. Tell her we ought to do dinner sometime," I said.

"I will, and we will. Take care and do your homework," he again directed.

After hanging up the phone I sat there thinking about what he told me. I spent a few minutes rewriting my notes so that I could read them at a later time. He was very helpful, as he always is.

Concept #6

Spend time determining what kind of legal structure works best for you and the business.

7

Decide and Move

"Well, someone told me it will take everything I have to start a business. Any thoughts?" I asked Dan the following week.

"I think it will take all of your time, talent, patience, nerves, emotional strength, and all of your money. It is a total commitment. If you don't commit totally, you will most likely fail," he responded.

The weather had cleared from the previous week. It was a glorious day, about nine in the morning. The birds were singing and actively looking for food. There was still a little dew on the grass so our shoes became wetter with each step and our clubs were as wet with each stroke, but the temp was near perfect. If there was any wind, it was just a whiff, not even enough to blow my hair. The sun was not fully over the mountain, so I had not yet put on my cap. I took several long deep breaths to take in as much of the morning air as I could. It was remarkable.

Today, we decided to drive a cart and play all eighteen holes, with the big boys, since we were cheated last week by the rain. Not as good of a workout, but our game would likely improve. We had played a few holes when I asked Dan about what I would have to commit to if, or when, I started my own business.

As we climbed back into the cart, Dan took a breath and said, "You know, sooner or later you will have to decide what kind of business to buy, what kind of legal structure it will be, and how you will finance the whole thing."

I sort of glanced at him as he drove down the cart path and responded, "Yes, I am coming to that realization. I am learning all about buying or starting a business, but without something to really sink my teeth into and analyze, all my knowledge gathering will not make any sense when there is nothing real to put it all to use. I've got to start seriously searching for something to buy. Got any ideas?" I asked him.

"Sure, ideas are what I am good at. The hard part is taking ideas and making something out of them. That will be your job this time around," he coached me.

All I could do was to nod my head in agreement. It was time for our second shot. Dan's ball was lying in the middle of the fairway, about one hundred sixty-five yards out. My lie was not as favorable. I was about two feet into the taller grass along the fairway and about fifteen yards behind his ball.

"Nice tee shot," I said, as I walked toward my ball.

"Lucky bounce," he responded.

As I was lining up my shot, I could not see the flag. "Is there a flag on the green?" I yelled.

"Yes, it is on the back of the green. I can barely see it from here," he responded.

"Oh, great! A blind shot, sort of like my new business venture. I am totally blind as to what I want to do," I thought to myself as I swung the club.

I was not focused on my shot, but thinking about a new business, any new business. I duffed the shot, and it dribbled down the fairway about fifty more yards.

"Too bad," Dan said under his breath.

"Yes, too bad," I scolded myself silently.

"Take your shot, and I will meet you up where mine landed," I directed.

After our two shots, both on the green, by the way, we climbed into the cart and Dan said, "Sooner or later you have to decide."

"Decide?" I questioned.

"Yes," he said. "Decide to decide. First you need to figure out what you want to do, what kind of business, then decide what kind of legal structure, and how you will begin. Will you buy a franchise or buy an existing business or start from scratch? But first, you need to be sure that it is what you really want to gamble on."

"You've been talking to me, and I hope to your wife," he probed.

"Yes, sure. We have been talking," I responded.

"Good. Talk to other friends and associates and family and trusted advisors and whoever else you can think of. Take what they say into consideration, but in the final analysis, you have to make the decision. You have to live with the results, good or bad," he said, emphasizing the word *you* each time he said the word.

It was finally sinking in and seemed to weigh heavier on me each time he pointed his conversation back to me.

"Yes. I need to decide. To make a decision and begin to move forward," I determined in my mind.

As we finished the round, there was not much more conversation regarding owning a business. I was trying to decide to decide in my own mind. That took my mind off my game, and my score showed the results.

"Not too good today," Dan observed.

"No, you got me thinking, and I was distracted," I responded.

"Yes. That was my intent, to get you to seriously think, make a decision and stop just talking and reading."

"Well, you accomplished your task," I told him.

"Great. Next week I want to hear what you decide to pursue," he ordered.

"I have decided to decide that very thing this week, and I will have your answer," I told him with just a little weight lifted off my shoulders.

Later that evening when Lori and I had gotten home from work, I told her about the conversation I had with Dan earlier in the day.

"Good for him," she said with some relief. "I was wondering if you were ever going to make up your mind. You are so, so indecisive sometimes."

"Tell me what you really think," I responded with irritation.

"I mean, you have talked about this for weeks now and I would like to see something a bit more tangible and something real to discuss. Planning is good and very important, but sometimes you can be difficult," she scolded.

"OK, OK, I have decided to come up with three good alternatives, make a comparison and weigh the pros and cons and make a decision. That is what I am going to do," I said with some finality in my voice.

Concept #7

Sooner or later you have to decide to decide.

8

What are the Options?

Over the next several days, I spent time searching the internet for ideas such as, businesses for sale, franchises that were available, and ideas that might be a good business to start up. Over the years I had some ideas that I thought would be winners and had narrowed it down to just a few, but after thinking about the obstacles of starting a business I determined not to go that route.

The ideas that I kicked around were a new phone app that could be used to sort and search posted jobs that were available. Then, there was a board game that a few friends and I thought about one evening while playing a few well known games. A third idea was a portable kind of desk that people with laptops could use instead of their laps. It would be big enough for a regular size laptop and maybe one or two other items, and could be used while sitting almost anywhere and have a hard surface for a mouse, and the other things.

The reasons I chose not to go it alone were many and varied and depended on what kind of new start-up I had contemplated. As always, everyone and his brother gave me loads of advice. Sometimes I felt like they thought I was crazy or stupid or just out to lunch. I should have asked a few people who actually had experience with a start-up, not people who did not have the grit to go for it personally.

If it were not for the following reasons, I might have really tried to do a start-up. It would have taken tons of patience and sacrifice, not to mention money and possibly my sanity. I could see many great advantages to doing a start-up, things like possible fame and fortune and just the sheer sense of accomplishment of doing something no one else had done or maybe even tried to do before. That would be a cool feeling. Here is a list of major hurdles that I believe I would have run into, that seemed too high for me to get over:

- Total dedication to the venture. A new start-up could require not having family, personal time, and other similar sacrifices.
- The venture could be un-bankable. Since it was an unproven endeavor, getting bank financing would be almost impossible.
- I did not want to get involved with venture capitalists. They would take a lot of the equity and want to be involved in many of the major decisions. It may prove cumbersome.
- Going small could mean a long time before I saw much of a return on any kind of investment, time, or money
- Some of the ideas I had would have taken computer developers, mechanical engineers, patent lawyers, and other extremely high paying contractors
- A start-up would take a much longer time to gestate, prove itself, and give me a payoff

Well, these are the major hurdles that I came up with and did not want to try and clear. I guess if I had an idea that was beyond the coolest thing in the world, it might make things more palatable, but I did not see any of my ideas as superhero kinds of ideas. They were good but not totally great beyond compare.

After deciding not to do a total new gig, I looked into many different kinds of franchises. There are hundreds and hundreds, maybe even thousands. Again, I decided not to go this route either. Many seemed like they would make good money but I found many reasons not to go this way, either. I won't go into all the different kinds of franchises that I looked into, but here are just the major problems that I felt I did not want to deal with:

- A franchise can be from fairly cheap to very expensive to get into. There are franchise fees, rent or buying land, and building a new building in compliance with a franchise agreement. Also, there could be equipment to buy and weeks of training somewhere that I did not want to be for two to four weeks.

- Usually, the franchisee is obligated to buy inventory, supplies, and other materials from the franchisor. In many cases, these goods have an abnormally high markup, more than you might pay to some other supplier, but it depends on the organization.
- The franchisee must pay an ongoing fee based on monthly sales and usually an additional fee for continuing advertising
- You are not really your own boss. The franchise must be run in accordance with the franchise agreement and just like every other operator in the chain of this particular business. Almost always, you must have the business open the hours that are dictated by the franchisor. You tend to have little leeway and almost no autonomy to run the business like you want. Basically, you are a glorified manager of someone else's store.
- When you want to get out of the business, there are various requirements involved that could limit any latitude while trying to unload a business

This was enough for me. I did not want to be so tied down to a business that I could not really run the way I wanted it to run. Don't get me wrong, there are many reasons why a person should buy a franchise, but it did not seem to fit my personality and my way of thinking. There are many reasons why you should buy some kind of franchise, but you will need to investigate those reasons yourself.

So (drum roll please) I decided to buy an existing business. That led me to other problems. Which business should I buy? Ok, so I spent a few more weeks speaking to many people, including a few business brokers. I found many kinds of businesses for sale. Everything from beauty salons to bars, but there were only a few entities for sale that I considered "real" businesses. I felt like I had a few talents like financial understanding, sales, and customer service and a knack for understanding people and what they really wanted.

Here are some of the parameters that I added to the check list to be sure I found something that would fit me, my personality, and goals:

- A business to business entity, one that dealt with other businesses and not a retail business
- It had to have actual assets that could be used as collateral in a bank loan situation
- The owner had to be willing to finance at least fifty percent of the purchase price
- It needed to have no client that was more than fifteen percent of total annual sales
- It had to have enough cash flow to pay me one hundred thousand per year in salary, if I chose to take that amount and enough additional cash flow to make monthly payments to a bank and/or the seller
- It needed to have a broad range of potential clients, extending into surrounding states and possibly foreign markets
- It had to be somewhat technical but not impossible because I felt I could afford a few highly trained technicians but not an entire company of them
- It had to have a potential to expand to where I eventually could work on the business and not just in the business
- It had to have enough appeal that would draw large investors and or buyers at some point in the future
- It had to be able to generate recurring revenue. (see appendix I)

Well, that was a lot of must haves. I didn't know if I could find something to fit all those parameters but I would try. If I gave up now, all my efforts would be just another exercise in futility. And I was tired of wasting so much time. Now I could focus my search efforts and match them against my check list. That sounded easy, right? No, not at all, it turned out to be a laborious task.

Concept #8

Find alternatives, weigh the options, and make a decision.

9

More Decisions

I missed golf the previous week because I had not completed the promise I gave to Dan the last time we played. I was sort of lucky in that the weather made for a good excuse not to play. This week however, I felt like I could face him with a sense of accomplishment. The sun was shining so I headed out to the links with a little excitement in my step.

Lori had bought me a new golf shirt. I thought I looked good in it or at least it looked good, so I wore it that day. It added even more spring in my pace.

I noticed Dan walking toward the Club House. "Dan. How's it going?" I asked as I met him in the parking lot, a few cars over from mine.

"I'm good, how about you?" he asked in return. "Well, did you keep your promise?"

I knew he would. He had nothing else to think about.

"Sure did." I responded with a self-assured tone in my voice.

"Great. Let's find our cart," he said, walking toward the Pro Shop.

Again, we decided to ride and play eighteen because of the week we missed.

"Number sixty-three," I declared. "There it is over next to the rock wall."

After checking with the starter, we loaded our clubs on the back of the cart and headed toward the first tee box. As the time before, the weather was marvelous. Just a little on the crisp side, but what a nice day.

In between the second and third hole Dan began to ask questions to be sure I had not been blowing smoke in the parking lot.

"Tell me about the progress you have made over the past few weeks," he asked pointedly.

I knew it was coming so I was ready. "I have decided to search for a business that is already in existence," I responded.

"Really?" he said. "Tell me how you came to that decision?"

"It wasn't easy," I began. "First, I made a list of things I wanted in a business, then, after a lot of research, I came up with the whys and the why nots of each type of business. Things like . . ." I then went into the reasons.

"That's a good method," Dan responded.

"That felt good," I thought.

I went on. "After going through the list on start-ups and franchises, I concluded that to obtain most of my criteria I needed to look for an existing business."

"Did you decide on a certain business to go after?" he then asked.

"Not totally, but I do think it needs to be some kind of service business because the capital outlay won't be as great as, say, a manufacturing concern," I went on. "I have found a few that I am researching, and it will be between an equipment repair business and a consulting outfit."

"That is awesome," Dan responded. "Now it is time to make a final determination. What are your parameters in making that kind of decision?"

I went through my list of the qualities I wanted in a business and then detailed some.

"In addition to those things we mentioned before, I want a company that has its accounts payable and receivables in good order, so I would not start behind or would have to collect a lot of old stuff. Second, I wanted a company where there was good potential of growing and using my skills for selling and finance. I think both of my finalists fit that category," I finished.

"Well then, what will be the deciding factor?" he asked.

"It will all boil down to the negotiations and the financing," I said.

"Makes sense."

"You're up," I said, feeling satisfied with my answers to him.

"No, you go ahead. You deserve it," he responded.

"Thanks," I said as I walked up on to the tee box.

After we both teed off, he peppered me with more questions.

"Have you thought about financing yet or begun a business plan? How about legal and accounting help? You know, there is more to buying a business than just saying you want to do it and looking on the internet to find one. There are many factors involved."

It was my turn to hit. What he said rattled me to the point that I duffed my fairway shot. It dribbled to the right about seventy five yards. "Ugh!" I mumbled under my breath.

"At least you didn't go into that tall stuff over there. It was close, but I think your lie is good," he responded.

I felt like smacking him upside the head, but I held my composure.

"No big deal. My next shot will be stunning," I told him, trying to remain positive.

"I hope so. You need to get close, so you don't get a double-bogie on this hole," he said, twisting the dagger a little.

"Yes, I know," I said, still holding my composure.

We finally finished up the round. The last four holes I was feeling better about myself. I still knew there was a lot to do, but really didn't want to be reminded of it on the golf course.

"Hey, sorry if I rattled your cage back there," Dan apologized.

"No big deal. I guess I was a little too self-assured about my progress," I responded.

"I am just here to help you. I don't want you to lose all of your confidence and money. I sort of like playing golf with you," he half kidded.

"I know you are trying to help. I am just a little overwhelmed with the process. I didn't realize it was going to take so much time, effort, and brain power," I said.

"Well, by next week you might have a little more progress. I will look forward to hearing about it. Have a great week," Dan said.

"Ok. I will keep you updated," I said, waving to him.

Concept # 9
It takes more than just a wish list and an internet search.
You must decide what to do and how.

10

What is the Deal?

The next week we were playing only nine and decided to walk. The weather was not as glorious as the week before, but it was Ok. When I arrived, I found Dan on the putting green practicing and waiting for me to arrive.

"Sorry, Dan," I exclaimed. "I got caught in a bit of traffic."

"No big deal. We are still waiting for the group in front of us to finish teeing off, and I wanted to sharpen my putting," He responded. "I'll try not to get you all riled up today. I'll go easy on the questions."

"Not a problem. Anyway, I have made a decision," I blurted out with some excitement in my voice.

"Wow, that is awesome! Tell me about it," he said. "We still have a few minutes before it is our turn."

"I decided to go after the equipment repair business," I stated with surety.

"Great. Tell me your reasoning," he directed.

"First of all, I did not pick the consulting firm because there were really no hard assets and I felt like the business was ninety plus percent on the current owner's ability and contacts," I began.

"Good thinking," he remarked quickly.

"It is not a done deal, but we have signed a letter of intent, which will give me 120 days to go through their books and do all my due diligence," I kept on. "It will give me time to meet a banker, prepare a loan package and do a business plan. You are the one who told me I needed all those things, right?" I said.

"Right. Keep going," he urged.

"The owner was real cool about everything. I spoke to his broker mostly but was able to meet the owner and visit for a while."

"Why is the guy selling?" Dan asked.

"He is over sixty and wants to slow down a little. He would like to stay on for a year or two to help make a good transition and for me to meet the customers. That sounds positive in my book," I noted.

"It is. With that kind of business, it is important to make a smooth transition," Dan said. "What else?"

"I really think there is potential to expand the business over time. The current owner is more of a technician and his wife does the books. I really don't think they manage the business as well as it could be done. I just think they go from crisis to crisis and put out fires all day long. It makes money, but it could do better, a lot better. I am sure of it," I said. "We have not decided on a price yet and all the other details, but I believe it is within my reach. I also think the owner wants to carry back a note, so he will be able to add to his retirement nest egg," I went on.

"Those are all good points. Maybe you have a winner here," Dan commented.

"I sure hope so. It sort-of plays to my strength for sales and customer relations. I can get the business side organized and spend time keeping customers happy and finding new ones. It might be fun," I said sort of running off at the mouth.

"One last thing." I continued. The company has maintenance contracts and generates recurring revenue. Right now, it is about 25% of the annual revenue but I am sure it can be increased."

By this time, it was our turn to begin the round of golf. We flipped a coin to see who teed off first. I won the toss. "It's my day," I stated.

"Go for it," he said.

Walking sort of took it out of me. I had spent a lot of extra time getting to where I was with the new business, and I was just tired. The last two holes did not go too well. I double bogeyed both. Not a good finish.

We still had some time, so we decided to get some lunch. The Grille had some pretty good food, and I wanted to visit with Dan a little more. I had a hundreds of things circling around in my head.

It was a little crowded, my head and the grill, but we found a table in the back. Not a very good view but quiet and where I could have Dan's undivided attention.

"How's this spot?" I asked.

"You know I like to look out the windows, but those tables are all taken and I am hungry. Let's take it," he responded.

After ordering two plates of the day's special, we began to explore more aspects of my project.

"I don't want to act like a school teacher but just a few questions, if you don't mind," he began.

"Sure. No problem. Just keep them simple. After those last few holes, I am still a little on the edgy side," I said.

"Do they rent space or own their location?" he asked.

"They are renting and have about two years left on the lease. Is that a problem?" I asked.

"No. That is actually good. It will give you time to get settled and time to find a new place if you don't like where they are now. How much are the current owners taking out to live?" he questioned.

"Combined is about one hundred K. That fits one of my parameters," I answered. "The current owner will need to be paid, but he will generate revenue so his income will be considered in a different manner. I will add this to the cash flow projections, when that time comes."

"If that time has not come, it should come real soon," Dan responded. "Next. What about the employees? Do they know the business is for sale and will they stay or go to a competitor?" he asked, winding up more questioning.

"They have all been very loyal to the current owner and yes, they know. He told them some time ago. I have not spoken to any yet, but that too is on my list of things to get done," I answered.

Lunch arrived, and it was a large plate of meatloaf. It looked great as the steam was rising off the plate and brown gravy oozed out all over the meat and the mashed potatoes. There was also a small side of broccoli to round off the meal.

"Wow! I was going to take Lori out for dinner tonight but that may have to be postponed. This is a big meal," I muttered.

By that time, Dan already had his mouth full of food. He looked content with the meal. After clearing his mouth of a large amount of food, Dan asked, "Do the employees have enough expertise to fix all the things that need fixing?"

"There are eight techs and two each specialize in specific kinds of equipment so there is back up, if needed. All of them have experience in most, if not all equipment serviced, but they like to specialize. The owner knows it all and is the cleanup hitter, if needed. He takes the things that are hard to fix and the machines that may be older and outdated," I told Dan. Lastly, with the eight techs I can leverage their assistance with the "multiplier effect. (See Appendix II for more detail on this.) I will need to focus on training to allow the owner to leave in a year or two. Maybe find a new 'cleanup hitter." I concluded.

"That is good. Tell me more," he requested.

"There are two office workers. One is the wife and the other is a young guy who has an Associates in Accounting. I think he is teachable, but I do not think his talents are fully utilized. He has excess capacity."

"Good, good. Do they own service trucks?" he then asked.

"There is one truck and one trailer, but the company pays mileage for the workers to travel to the customer's locations in their own vehicles. The guy says it is cheaper that way. I will do a short analysis to see if it really does save money," I told Dan.

"There are a lot more questions to be asked, but I really need to head out. I have to go see the dentist. Not really looking forward to this visit," Dan said, cutting off my next sentence.

"Yes, I need to run myself. I have missed too much work and the boss has given me the look. You know what I mean?" I asked.

"Ok, see you next time," Dan said as he got up from the table. "I will check on your progress in a week. You have a lot of homework to get done. Take care and good luck, pal," Dan said adding a little bit of anxiety.

"Right, see you next week," I said.

Concept #10

The work begins in earnest after coming to a decision.

11

Have a Good Plan

My time earlier in the day with Dan made realize that I had piles of things that I needed to get done while I was negotiating the purchase of the business, Medical Equipment Repair, Incorporated or MERI for short. My mother's name was Mary, which helped me remember. Actually, she was a little flattered when I told her the short name of the company. It was a fun thing to kid around with her from time to time about it. My dad was not as thrilled with my antics.

That evening Lori and I went to our favorite Chinese place where Charlie worked. This time however, we ordered our own plates, which pleased me very much. I had the Mongolian beef, and she had the Moo Goo Gai Pan again. "Glad I got to order my own," I thought.

While we were waiting for our food to be served, we began to discuss all the things that had to be done to make this venture a reality.

"Why don't you take all the ideas that are racing around your brain and write them down?" Lori said.

"That is exactly what I need to do, develop a good business plan," I responded with a smile.

While the food was being placed on the table, I began to think back to a college capstone class I had that required us to write several business plans. I determined to go home that evening and find what I had done.

"You know, I think I have a copy of a plan I did in college," I told Lori. "I even think I have it in an electronic version somewhere on my computer."

"Well now, aren't I smart?" Lori said with satisfaction. She asked a few questions about what it needed, and from memory I gave her a small list of items.

"If my memory serves me well, it needs to have things like a description of the business, a good mission statement, and financial projections. Since this is a going business it will need to have copies of the prior year's financial information," I rattled off.

"You don't remember all of that. You must have been through this earlier today," she said in a questioning tone.

"No, really. I just happen to remember those items," I said, trying to convince myself, too.

"What else Mr. Smarty Pants?" she teased.

"Let's see. Maybe we need to put in things about personnel biographies, location description, list of equipment and, well, I am sure there are other things. I think with different kinds of businesses, the items needed in a business plan can change, too." I said, finishing up my memory dump.

"I took a look on the internet and found oodles of different plans. One to fit every occasion. Just like all those handbags in your closet," I said with a dig.

"Don't even go there, pal."

Dinner was great. Charlie and I bantered a little, as we normally do. I had begun to feel better now that I had a plan to write up a real business plan and unload my mind of all the details. I would also need to make a master "Things to Do" list to help me organize and remember all of the various steps and tasks that needed to be done.

I felt so much better. We agreed to split a desert.

"Which one do you want?" I asked.

"There is not much of a selection. Fortune cookies and some kind of custard thing is all I see," she said with a bit of disappointment.

"Pick one or we can stop for ice cream down the street," I responded.

"No, I'm good. A fortune cookie is good enough. Maybe it will tell us if you should go out on your own or not," she said whimsically.

"I'm kind of full, anyway. Let's get the check and hit the road," I suggested.

The check came with two fortune cookies. I opened mine and read out loud, "Your luck is about to change."

"I told you it would give us the answer, now didn't I?" Lori said in a immodest manner.

"You are always right," I said, with a bit of a puzzled look on my face.

When we got home after dinner, I got on my computer to see if I could find one of those old business plans.

"Honey, look at this," I called with excitement. "Not only did I find one, I found hundreds of them on the internet."

I couldn't believe how many and how varied they were. Now the hard part would be to pick the one that fit my business and my style. "MERI is going to get a nice, new plan," I determined to myself.

"The cookie was right, my luck is changing," I said, still speaking to myself.

Lori began to work on a craft project she had started earlier in the week. I began to look at plan after plan. Finally, after an hour or so, I made a decision. It was not only going to be thorough, but also it was going to look good too. I was still feeling good. It had been a great day.

Concept #11

A business plan is a must.

Get the ideas out of your head and on paper.

12

Help and Advice

That evening and into the next day, I worked on the plan as much as I had time. I got to one part that spoke of various positions, such as, Chief Financial Officer, Chief Operating Officer, and several others. I did not need and would not be able to afford a team of highly paid executive level employees. As I sat there thinking about it, I remembered something Dan had mentioned a few weeks back. He told me to find a lawyer, an accountant, an IT person, a human resource specialist, a marketing expert, and a few other notable consultants.

"That's it!" I thought. "I will find friends and or get referrals from friends and ask them to sit on a special advisory board to help me with special circumstances. I could not pay them much, but if, say I needed a lawyer, then I could use the one that sat on my Advisory Board and pay for services rendered. Likewise, with an accountant and all the others. I hoped that I could sell them on the idea that as I grew, their roles could increase and they could be part of something special, a growing and expanding venture. It would not hurt to ask. It would cost nothing to ask them, now would it?"

I got on the internet and looked up "Advisory Boards" and found that this format is a more casual non-paid group of consultants or advisors. No legal liability for them unless I actually hired them for a specific task.

"Dan is right. It does seem like a great idea," I told myself. "I may even ask Dan to sit on the board. He has been an advisor and mentor so far. Maybe he would like it. I will ask him the next time we play."

I called Lori to tell her about this idea. She thought it was a very good idea.

"Maybe I can sit on the Advisory Board and be your marketing specialist. After all, that's what I do," she said convincingly.

"Yes, and I can ask Wally if he wants to be the legal advisor. Awesome, that is three so far who I think will work. I think it will really help me make major decisions and get different perspectives," I said.

"Who else can you get for this little group?" Lori asked.

"Let's see, you, Wally, Tim, the banker friend of mine. That's three, who else?" I thought out loud.

"How about Dan? Think he would throw his hat into the ring?" she asked.

"That is an obvious one." I responded with excitement in my voice. "I still need an IT person, maybe a practitioner who uses the equipment, an HR specialist, and maybe a CPA. I will think about what specialties I will need."

"Well, add all this to your "Things to Do" list so you don't forget," she urged.

"You know, I remember Dan telling me that we should have meetings on a regular basis, monthly at first and then quarterly when I get my feet on the ground. I could bring lunch in for the group to at least offer them something," I responded.

"Yes. That is what I will work for, lunch. Deal!" she said, holding out her hand for me to shake.

I sort of brushed it away and just said, "Watch it, girl."

Lori went back to her little project, and I hurriedly went back to my business plan project and added to the list of all the things that needed to be done. It kept growing.

Concept #12

Put a team of advisors together. You will need the help.

13

Negotiations

I had been negotiating for almost a month, and we finally came to an agreement in concept. All I had to do was to sign the contract, pay some earnest money, find a loan for the remainder of the purchase, price and begin to run the business. There were still a lot of things left on my "To Do" list but many of them would be done once the business was mine, or at least mine and the bank's.

I went in to work the next day and gave my two weeks' notice. That was hard. Several of my co-workers already knew. My boss had an idea that something was up. Because I was at a financial institution, that day would be my last. They asked me to clean out my personal belongings and agreed to pay the two weeks and the accumulated commissions that I had earned. That was a nice surprise, to say the least.

Lori was all in and called me later in the morning to give me some encouragement.

"How did it go, Hun?" she asked, searching for my feelings.

"It went well, and I am almost out of here. They are paying me for the two weeks but do not want me to mingle with clients or employees right now. They were good about things, I think," I responded.

"Did you finalize the plan last night?" she asked.

"It was late, but yes, it is done. I now need to complete a loan package for the bank. I have about two weeks until closing the purchase, but the banker is confident that the timing will all work out," I told her. "I will spend the rest of the day and tomorrow getting it done."

"Good job. Now, I really need to head into my meeting. I will talk to you later," she said.

After saying goodbye to my friends and fellow workers, I headed home to work on the bank's requested items. There were lots of things they needed. Things like a personal financial statement, copies of my last two years of tax returns, past financial statements from MERI, a copy of my business plan with projections and many other personal kinds of information. They gave me a comprehensive list and many were part of my newly completed business plan so it did not to require additional work on my part.

I was lucky to be familiar with the finance world, at least for most kinds of financing. I thought about different ways to come up with money. Here is a brief list of some of the methods that I had considered for funding my new venture.

- Personal savings – I had a good chunk, but not enough for the entire purchase price
- Friends and family money – I did not want to cause strains in any of my personal relationships. I did not want to go that route. It was not for me or any friends or relatives. It has worked for many over the years, however.
- Crowd Funding – This was an option, but required a stellar marketing campaign and had not been widely used to buy exiting business. I almost went that way; however, but after discussing it with a few people I decided not to. It was not my style.
- Bank loan – Since MERI was an existing ongoing business, this made sense to me and my banking contracts, one of which I had asked to be on my Advisory Board.
- Private Investor – This was a real option but might take a bit more time to find the right person, and then it could get awkward if things did not go well.
- Venture Capital – The purchase of MERI was too small for this method. It is in the back of my mind if things go well in the future and if my plan to grow the business works out.

There were other ways, but the internet outlined all in great detail. It warned to be careful not to go with just anyone as there are many scammers in the wings just waiting to take advantage of the innocent. Trust me. I've seen it.

One day, while talking to my banker friend, I was blessed with some good advice.

In each of these options one of the main instruments for an investor/banker is to look at a good, well-thought out set of Cash Flow projections.

Tim Brooks, my banker friend had been through this drill many times. He had made a few loans over the years and had turned down many also. He was a seasoned pro.

Tim began the normal banker instruction. "The reason why cash flow projections are so important is because they are used to help us determine if the business will be able to make payments, pay bills, etc. In your case, you have existing numbers that gives you a base to start from. That will make life easier for you and for us. All you will need to do is to change a few of the line items and give your best guesstimate as to how you plan to make things big, better, faster, cheaper, so to speak."

"You mean that I will be guessing?" I asked him.

"Yes. You don't really know for sure how things will work out. It is a guess, and in this case it will be an educated guess, based on the history of the company," he told me.

"Of course, I knew this but I wanted him to feel good about his position," I thought.

"As you add or delete staff, add a salary for you and delete the current owner's pay and other things like that, the numbers will change slightly. Other items to think about will be new sales revenue from your efforts to find new clients. So just take each line item on the sample I will give you and customize the spreadsheet with the items that fit this business. It is really not that hard," he stated with some conviction. "You can even find different formats on the web, if you don't like this one. One last important detail is to be sure you carry the cash balance from one period to the next so that you will have a good estimate of how much cash will be on hand."

He concluded with assurance and conviction, "You know the old saying, right? 'Cash is King!' Don't ever forget it. You can grow the business right out of existence. If your sales go up, you need more cash to pay for parts and labor, etc. If you have no cash to do this, then you cannot satisfy the customers. We will discuss this later, once you have given me more information. Again, cash is extremely important. It also makes us bankers feel better too."

"I will remember that," I said as I got up from the desk to leave. "Cash is King. Got it!"

Concept #13

A good and complete loan package and business plan is a must in order to obtain a loan or funds from almost any kind of investor.

RUNNING YOUR BUSINESS

14

Cash Flow

I arrived home that evening just in time to catch Lori before she left to run some errands.

"Where you headed?" I asked.

"I have about five places I need to hit before the evening is over. Want to come along?" she said.

"Sure. But you have to get me some food. I talked to Tim today, and he gave me some assignments to work on. I will tell you all about them," I responded.

"Hop in. I'll drive. I know where I need to go and you can talk," she said with a smile on her face.

"What did 'ol Timmy have to say, anyway," she began as the car moved forward.

"Cash flow. That is what we discussed. Cash flow," I told her.

"OK, go on. I'm listening," she encouraged.

"Actually, we ended up talking about cash flow and cash flow statements, but he spent most of the time trying to help me figure out what my contribution to the business would be. What my expertise is and how I can make MERI bigger, better, faster, cheaper. Actually, make it more profitable through various improvements," I replied.

"Do you have any skills to contribute?" she again quipped.

"You are in one of those moods, aren't you?" I asked.

"I don't know. I feel pretty good and had a productive day," she came back.

"How was it so productive?" I asked, trying to be interested in her work.

"Mostly the usual, but I received a few compliments and it made me feel good," she offered.

"Awesome. Tell me about it," I said.

"Well, I think that we, my boss and I, have figured out that I have a few skills that she does not have and that she likes how I handle some things. It made me feel good to know I can do things that no one else in our little company can do," Lori continued.

"Awesome! Nice going," I congratulated her. "I think I have also found what I can do with the new company that no one else can do."

"That is sort of what I think I have figured out for my place in MERI. I can sell and make clients feel good about hiring us. I can also understand the money needs and cash movement that needs to take place," I said to her.

"I can attract and maintain customers too, but you know I am not really good with the finances, so tell me a little," she requested.

"OK, here goes. I will spend one half of my time calling on and servicing customer accounts. The company is not doing this currently. As it is now, they let the service techs do the customer contact and many of them do not have the most outgoing personalities. Of course, I will begin this once I have a handle on the accounting, the systems that are in place and getting to know the employees, etc. Then there is the managing of the cash. Tim believes that cash is one of the most important ingredients in a business and that examining it should be done correctly and often. If we ever run out of cash, we will not be able to buy parts or pay the techs to fix things."

At this point I took a breath, and Lori said, "Wow. I wonder who does that in our company."

"In most small companies, it is the owner or the spouse of the owner. It is that important. Also, there have been many stories where a trusted employee needs a little extra cash and figures out a way to take it with no one knowing. Sooner or later they get caught but it can take years before that can happen," I told her, sort of quoting Tim. "One other thing I need to do is to collect the accounts receivable in a timely manner."

"Why so?" she said as she pulled into the parking lot of a store that she needed to visit. "Hold that thought, and I will be right back."

While she was in the store, I went back and read some of the notes that I had taken when Tim and I talked. It was a good reminder and helped me with the next part of our discussion.

"Find everything?" I asked as she got back into the car.

"I sure did. That is a great store. Now, you were telling me about some kind of accounts something," she probed.

"Accounts receivable. It is the money that is owed to the company by the customers for work that was done," I explained.

"Oh, I get it," she responded. "Go on. With this traffic it will take a few minutes to get to the next stop."

"Anyway, if you don't put forth the effort to collect the AR's as they can be called, the customers take their time to pay. Usually, you give the customer thirty days or so to pay, but some have their own cash flow problems and tend to ride whomever they can for as long as they can. It becomes a vicious cycle. One that I do not want to be part of," I said in a stern tone. "So, if we don't collect our AR's, then we have to slow pay some of our suppliers or rent or even not pay the employees on time."

"Now that would be horrible," Lori piped in. "Hope that doesn't happen in my office."

"The same thing can happen with spare parts. MERI does not have to carry a lot of inventory, but some companies need to carry finished goods or raw materials and too much can mean trouble. Both too much inventory and long collection cycles for AR's can eat up a lot of cash and cause big problems and even put some companies out of business. A company like that can be rich in assets but with no cash, bad things can happen," I said trying to finish up.

"So, to sum it up, cash flow is a very important component in all companies, especially small ones like MERI. Collect accounts receivable in a timely manner and keep just enough inventory on hand."

Concept # 14

Manage your cash closely.

Collect your accounts receivable.

Keep the right amount of inventory.

15

Contributing

All the cash flow discussion was interesting, but I was still concerned with what my contribution would be. It kept me up most of that night trying to figure it out. Too bad too, because I had a sun-up golf date with Dan and showed up late. The first couple of holes were fairly disastrous. I was stiff, my swing was labored, and the ball did not seem to know where to go. It was not my best round, to say the least.

Dan was trying to console me. As we walked down the next fairway he noticed that I was preoccupied.

'What's up with that swing of yours?" he questioned.

"I was up all night worrying how I was going to make my upcoming investment turn into gold," I responded.

"Gold?" he questioned in surprise. "Are you talking about your new business purchase?

"Yes, how do I make all the puzzle pieces fit together?" I asked, as he chuckled under his breath. "I have always heard the old saying, 'if it is to be, then it is up to me.' You ever heard that one?" I asked him.

"Sure I have. It is an old saying, but I think you have the wrong understanding about it," he asserted. "I think that applies, but only to a certain extent. When you are running a business it is more like leading an orchestra. You direct the whole group of players, but you are not the expert of each instrument. You don't play them all, but it is your job to make sure everyone does his part, in harmony with all the others. In business, that is how it is. You will play a role or two, but if you try to do everything, you will never grow and your employees will be frustrated and go somewhere else. They want to contribute and play their own instruments. They want to feel needed. We all do. It is human nature. I think this is exactly what you are feeling now."

"Ok. So I don't need to stress out over it? I asked.

"Not at all. Embrace it and learn to make it work for you and the business," Dan responded.

"How do I figure out all that?" I asked him.

"It will come. Find out each employee's strengths and duties and then fill in the gaps. You will need to use your financial and sales skills to your advantage, but certainly you have no clue how to fix one of those machines. Don't even go there," he said in a somewhat authoritative tone.

"I think I get it," I responded.

"Even if you know how to do a certain task, let whoever's job it is do it. It is their responsibility and that person knows what is expected, then just get out of their way. Let them sink or swim. Usually it will be swim. Most people really want to succeed and show their stuff, so to speak," he said.

"I asked myself how he knew all of this. He was pretty amazing," I thought.

He started up again. "One of the goals is to get the business to run itself so you don't have to be there all the time. You need a vacation too. You will want to sell the thing someday, and if it is all about you, then it is not very saleable. Look at the current owner. He never gets time off and is burned out, so all he knows what to do is to sell it. Am I right?" he questioned concluding his comments.

"I think you are right. I do believe that is why it is for sale and why I am getting, in my option, such a good deal on the purchase," I said.

"Exactly. Some owners figure it is too hard to teach and show others how, or they think that no one can do it better than them. That is a bad assumption, and it stunts growth and employee satisfaction. Don't do it," he instructed again.

"I think I get to tee off. I did win that last hole," Dan said, demeaning my performance on the last hole. As he hit the ball, it flew way to the right.

"Nice shank!" I barbed him after he hit one into the weeds. "I didn't get any sleep last nigh, and I can do that good. Let me hit, and we will go see if we can find that ball of yours."

As we walked toward the direction the ball headed, Dan began a little more instruction. "One more thing you need to think about is that you have to hire people you can trust. If you don't trust them don't hire them or keep them, even for the smallest tasks. It just won't work over the long term," he advised.

"What about the ones who are already there?" I asked.

"That can be a little bit harder. Give it time. Get to know them, but if they have been there for any length of time, they should be Ok or your predecessor would not have kept them," he told me.

"That makes sense. But what about me?" I asked with what must have been a puzzled look on my face.

"You will work toward your strengths and if you don't want to or can't do something, you will have to fill in those gaps. It will come to you pretty quickly," he counseled.

"Remember you are the conductor of the orchestra. Bring them together and make beautiful music together. Or at least make the place run smoothly so the work will get done. It will be challenging, but you will have fun doing it," he finished up as we walked up on the green. "Nice chip."

Concept # 15

You need employees you can trust.

Then, let them do their work and succeed.

16

Changing Hands

The sale closing day came and I was still on the nervous side. I had Lori go with me to Wally's office to sign the papers and hand over the down payment. I had a three prong financing approach. I put in what I could and had a bank lend me as much as they were willing and the owner financed the remaining portion. I believe it worked out well for me and the seller.

"Wow, I'm still a little nervous," I confessed to her.

"Let's just go through your list to be sure you have all your ducks in a row," she recommended.

"Good idea. Let's see, I have the loan package done and to the bank. The bank loan is approved and ready to fund. My cash flow projections look great. I have put my advisory council together and ready for the next meeting. What am I missing?" I asked her.

"Well, you know your legal structure. You have decided to make it an S Corp, which will allow you to move the taxes into our personal tax return. Also, you have met all or most of the employees and seem to have won them over to your way of running the company. You know what they do and what they are good at doing. You have an adequate amount of cash to work with and a small revolving bank loan, if needed. And you have me. You best supporter," she concluded with a smile on her face and an encouraging look.

"That's right. You are really all I need. The business is just a means to an end," I said as I squeezed her hand gently.

"OK, then. No need to worry. Your tie is even straight, and Dan is a phone call away if you need his advice," Lori added.

"One thing I have done over the past few days is develop a dashboard of indices that I want to see on a daily or weekly basis to be sure I am on track," I told Lori.

"Explain it to me. I haven't heard of it before," she responded.

"The last time Dan and I played golf, we stayed after and ate lunch. Remember I had that chicken fried steak that I told you about?" I reminded her.

"Yes, I remember that but not the dashboard thing," she said. "Explain it to me."

"It consists of about four to six numbers that I need to know to be sure the business is on track. So far, I want to know on a weekly basis my cash balance, bills coming due that week, projected accounts receivables that should come in, and that sort of thing," I said ticking them off using my fingers to count each.

"How is it a dashboard?" Lori asked.

"Just like the dashboard in your car, you can quickly look down and see how fast you are going, how much gas you have, the battery charge, and the engine temperature. Sometimes there are more things to look at and sometimes less. It really depends on the needs of the driver, or in this case, the needs of the business," I responded.

"Well that makes good sense. I like the idea," Lori replied with her approval.

"Many business use financial ratios such as the quick ratio, the current ratio, accounts receivable collection period, inventory turnovers per year and others. There is a ratio for almost anything. I looked on the internet and found many of them, with definitions. It was really massive. I don't need the inventory ratio, but I do need the A/R ratio and the quick and current ratios because they deal with my cash position. I also need to know what work is scheduled for the day and the following five day period to help plan the tech's routes," I said as we pulled up to Wally's office.

As we walked in, I finished up my primer on dashboards. "The contents of the dashboard depend on the things that are important to the specific business. It needs to be customized," I concluded.

"I will ask my boss if they use a dashboard. It makes total sense to me. Now, take a deep breath, exhale slowly, and be on your game," Lori encouraged.

Wally's admin greeted us in the lobby.

"He is waiting for you in the conference room," she said sweetly and directed us away from the door.

"Well, if it isn't the proud parents," Wally said with a grin on his face.

"Parents?" Lori said with some objection.

"You know. Soon to be the proud parents of a business."

His words made my heart skip a little beat. The nervousness began to build.

"Please. Have a seat," he said, motioning for us to sit across the table from his chair. "It looks like everything is in order. We have all the documents ready to go, and as soon as you sign and hand over all that money, it will almost be done. The owner is on his way, and as soon as I am finished with him, he will hand over the keys, so to speak. You better be ready for the first day on the job Monday." My heart beat even faster.

Today was Friday, and it would give me the weekend to make my plan for my first day and first week. The owner offered for me to come a week ahead of time, but I did not feel right and wondered what all the employees would think, so I waited until after the actual closing. I hope it was the right decision. I would soon find out.

We were fairly quiet on our ride home. We had done everything we needed to do, and now we were just waiting for a call from Wally to tell us that it was a done deal. I kept looking at my silent cell phone. "No lights, no sound, no nothing," I kept saying to myself.

Lori sensed my anxiety and began some small talk about the weather or something. I wasn't really listening.

A mile or so from home my phone finally rang. It was Wally.

"Well," he said, "you are proud parents of MERI. Congratulations. I hope you will be merry this weekend. Get it? Just a bad attempt at humor. I will be in touch. Go celebrate or something, because you will need to be on your game next week. Good luck."

Lori could hear his voice and reached over and gave me a big one on the cheek.

"Now all you have to do is to make it work for us. I know you can, honey," she said in her most positive voice.

"I will give it everything I have," I told her. Then I thought about that saying, "if it is to be, then it is up to me."

Yes, I was excited and nervous, all at the same time. I needed some chill time.

Concept # 16

Develop a dashboard to help you manage the business day to day.

17

Everything

I finally settled down after a nice dinner and then went to a local high school football game. I yelled so hard, I forgot about my new baby, the business. It had been a long day and I hit the sack early. Besides, I had a golf match with Dan the next morning, Saturday.

We were going to play the big boys' course, all eighteen holes. Since it was a busy day, the starter paired us up with two other guys. I had seen them around, but did not know them well, or even at all. Dan didn't know them either.

I probably should not have been playing golf and spend the time focusing on my business, but walking nine holes took only about two hours and the club was on the way between home and the shop. Besides, it helped me keep sane. Dan's advice was important to me, and that was the only place he would give it for free. That was why I played.

In golf, there is a lot of idle chatter when you begin play. We played the question and answer thing for the first few holes. I really think I lucked out, however. One guy was an ex-banker, and his cart mate had owned his own business but had sold it a few years back. I just needed to figure out how to cross examine them in a way that would not feel awkward to me or them. By this time, Dan was already into peppering questions at them. He told them what I had done the day before, and it seemed to pique their interest. Anyway, it gave us something to talk about besides my bad shots. It was a nice diversion.

"So you bought a medical equipment repair business yesterday?" the banker said. "Good luck to you."

"Thank you," I responded humbly.

"I owned a distribution business for many years," said his golf partner. "My advice to you is that you need to know your business from top to bottom, you know, from A to Z."

"He is right," the banker piped in. "You have to know or you will lose track, and it will kill you and the business."

"How do you both suggest I do that?" I questioned. Dan was just standing there with a bit of a smile on his face, listening attentively.

"Here is what I would do," began the business owner. "I would get to know each and every employee first and figure out how good they are and how honest, too. Then, I would go to all of the larger clients and introduce myself and offer my help any time of the day or night. Find out what they wanted and needed and get them to trust and count on you and your company. That's where I'd start."

Mr. Banker then began, "I would make sure I knew where my cash was at all times. Who owed me money and what money I owed and to whom. And, never get behind in your bills. It can be a real killer."

"Those are great suggestions," I commented, looking from one to the other.

"You're up, my businessman," Dan said to me, breaking up the chatter.

It was a par five and so I swung as hard as I could, still thinking about what they had told me. The ball dribbled out in front of the tee box about thirty yards or so.

From behind me, I heard, "Take a deep breath and relax. You have until Monday to make it all happen."

Those were not comforting words at all. I did take a deep breath and hit a second tee shot, but this time it flew at least three hundred yards, straight down the fairway.

"There you go," encouraged Dan. "That is what you need to do in your business. Take a deep breath and do the best you can. Nothing to stress about, really."

We were all on the green heading toward our various ball locations, when I asked, "What other suggestions do you two have to offer?"

"I will tell you as soon as I sink this putt," said the ex-banker.

"Nice putt," said his partner, as the ball landed in the bottom of the cup.

"That's my partner. I'll keep him."

The banker's partner, feeling good after his cart mate drained the putt, began, "I would go on service calls and figure out how long each take and how they are handled. That way when something goes wrong, and it will, you will better understand what happened and why and maybe how to fix the problem."

Then the banker butted in, "I would understand the accounting system, how jobs are booked etc. and then figure out if there is a way to increase productivity. Since you get paid by the customers for hours on the job, it is important to know how to schedule things so there is as little dead time as possible."

Then it was Dan's turn. "Again, what they say is good and important. You must understand every aspect of your business, from A to Z, so you can better control what happens. You need to make the business bigger, better, faster, cheaper. To repeat what I have told you earlier. You need to grow it so it will become a good investment for you in the long run. You will someday want to or need to sell the thing and you want to sell if for more than you bought it, plus inflation. That is really the bottom line."

"Good advice," they both said in unison, as we headed toward the next hole.

A few holes later, the ex-banker began a speech about keeping up with the markets and news in general.

"I read the *Wall Street Journal* every day, religiously. It helps me know what is happening in the world like new trends, products, and services. It keeps me up to date," he said.

"I also like the local business news and scour the news pages on the internet. Not the off-beat pages but the more well-known and trustworthy selections. One more thing is that I would read everything I could about the industry that my business belonged to. I would subscribe to trade magazines and attend tradeshows and other learning opportunities," said the banker's cart partner.

Finally, it seemed like it was Dan's turn to offer his view point. "Let's finish strong," he offered.

Concept #17

Know the business from A to Z. It is your life blood.

18

Getting to Know You

It was finally Monday, my first official day at my own business. I got to the office very early, only to find a couple of the techs talking and drinking a cup of coffee. I didn't know who had keys to what and it sort of perplexed me because it was like pulling teeth for me to get a set of keys from the prior owner. I guess I had a lot to learn.

"Hey, guys!" I blurted out in an upbeat voice.

"Ah, hi Mr. ah, ah . . ." he stammered because he had forgotten my name.

"It is, well, just call me boss. I need that right now. I am a little nervous," I confessed to them both.

"Actually, we are too, boss. We all are nervous not knowing what is going to happen," one of them said.

"It is a big change for us. We have been here a long time and felt pretty secure, but now our little world has been shaken. You know what I mean?" he asked.

"I think I do know what you mean," I responded. "I worked at a place once that was bought out by a larger company and actually lost my job. It was no fun. No one needs to worry about losing their jobs. I need you all here, because, guess what? I don't know how to fix anything. Not even my cell phone."

They both just laughed and seemed to relax.

"Really now, I need you both to help me through my long learning curve and teach me the business. I think I may even have a few ideas to make it better and more productive," I added. "Wouldn't both of you like to see things get better?"

"We sure would," they both said at the same time.

"We have some ideas that may help if you give us a chance," one of them said.

"OK, then. That is just what we are going to try and do. Maybe even start an incentive plan where you can earn a little extra in your paychecks. How does that sound?" I questioned them as I looked for signs of excitement.

The older guy exclaimed, "Now that's the kind of thing we have wanted for some time now. How will it work?" he asked.

"I don't know yet, but we will figure it out. Guaranteed," I promised.

They both smiled.

During our conversation, some of the other workers began to arrive. I had scheduled a meeting at 8 am to introduce myself, answer questions, and try to make a good beginning.

Once everyone had arrived, we began our meeting. They introduced themselves and told me a little about their families, and I did the same thing. Then I opened it up for questions and suggestions.

This was probably the best thing I could have done, because it gave them an opportunity to verbalize their feelings and concerns and gave me a lot of good ideas for improvement. Of course, I had paper and a pen to record the ideas that they gave me.

It was obvious that several of the quieter folks had little to nothing to say during this group session. I would sooner or later find out what everyone was thinking, I hoped.

Throughout the day, I had a one-on-one meeting with everyone to hear them out and to get to know them on a more personal level. It was a busy day, filled with hope for a new beginning.

The very next day, after things settled down somewhat, I outlined an incentive plan for each person. I really believe in paying for performance and hoped to instill a sense of ownership with each person's specific job. Most were very pleased with the prospect of adding to their pay checks. I figured this would garner a lot of new ideas, methods, and other ways to improve the overall running of the business. It was fun to see a new sense of life in an old company.

I did see some bewilderment coming from the prior owner. He had stayed, but I was not sure he approved of my new ideas. "I will win him over," I vowed to myself.

The following week, we met for another employee meeting to go over some of the changes that they had mentioned and a few of my own. We again began at 8 am and had pushed the first stops out an hour or two.

"Thanks to everyone for coming today and for the cooperation you have given this past week. I really appreciate the effort," I opened.

I took questions first to allow those with questions to be sure they were heard and to be sure they were not distracted from my upcoming comments. This format worked well, and we used it at our monthly meetings thereafter.

I do not have space or time to recount the entire meeting but have a list of my notes and promises that I took and made during this second meeting.

- Establish an employee incentive program, based on individual production and overall company success
- Set up and begin a 401k plan for each person and put in a contribution matching percentage
- Formalize a PTO plan to allow each employee to have paid time off for vacation and sick leave
- Improve the health care coverage
- Explore our competitor's employee benefits and equal or match those to the best that we could
- Establish an organizational structure so everyone knows the proper chain of command
- Formalize a procedure manual and better define what was expected, so each person knows what is required

- Do a study of the work flow to be sure you have the correct personnel in the right job and that all functions are adequately covered with backups in case of sickness or work overload

At the end of that meeting, and throughout the following week, everyone seemed to be very pleased and happy with the proposed changes and ideas. I really did not know how we would pay for some of these things, but the idea that they were in play meant a lot to most of my workers.

Concept #18

Take good care of your employees.

19

Intruders

One morning about five o'clock I received a call from our security provider. They did not know what was happening, but it forced me to throw on some clothes and head into the shop.

"Where are you going?" my wife said because she was awakened by the phone call.

"That was Security Seven. They told me that things are not right, but they didn't know what it was, so I need to head down there to find out. It can't be a break in. We don't really have much to steal. Just a bunch of old machines and parts. It's probably nothing," I told her as she rolled over.

"Call if you need anything," she mumbled.

There was not much traffic, so I made it in record time, only to find, well, nothing.

"What the heck? I got up early for this?" I scolded myself.

A few days later I arrived at the shop to find that all of our systems were down or not working well. It was not too big of a problem because all we had at that point were our accounting system, our website, and a program that helps with ordering parts and shows diagrams of how to fix all of the various pieces of equipment that we may come across.

The previous owner had a contract with some IT firm to manage all of our online needs, but I had not met them yet. Maybe it was time to have them come over and check things out.

The next day, at the prescribed time, one of the IT company's techs show up in his little car, which was all covered with some kind of see through advertising wrap like material that mostly covered his entire car. He introduced himself as Matt Morrison. He was wearing a nice shirt that showed his company's logo embroidered over the pocket. He seemed like a decent, sharp guy. I was actually impressed, even though I was expecting some kind of geeky dude with thick glasses or some wild get up. Anyway, he gave a very good impression.

As a side note, I immediately felt that his appearance and the IT's system of dressing its cars and employees was exactly what MERI needed to do to help promote good customer service and the business in general. I took note for later consideration.

"What seems to be the problem?" Matt explored, sort of like a doctor trying to diagnose what was wrong with your health. I liked his approach and style. I took another note to be sure my Techs were consulted as well.

"Well, our systems have been up and down. Sometimes they work and sometimes not so good," I told him.

"Can you give me an example?" he asked.

We went back and forth asking and answering questions to try and figure things out. We talked about who has access to what and different security settings and passwords and that kind of thing. Most of the questions were technical. I did not feel like I had great answers, but Matt did not let me know that I didn't know what I was talking about.

"One more thing," I said, holding up my hand like a policeman trying to get a driver to stop his car.

"What's that?" Matt asked.

"Last week at about five in the morning I received a call from our security company who told me that things were not right at the office, but they could not pin down the problem. So, I put my clothes on and came in, only to find nothing," I told him.

"Well that is strange," he commented as he sat down and began to enter various keystrokes on the keyboard.

"I'll come check on you later," I told him, as I headed out to the shop to be sure the guys were moving toward their assigned stops.

Not too much time had passed, and Matt came looking for me.

"Well, I have some good news and some not so good news," he said hesitantly.

"Now is as good as any. Lay it on me," I instructed.

"I think your system was somehow hacked last week. That has caused the current problems that you are experiencing," he told me.

"Hacked?" I blurted out. "How can that be? Why would anyone want to hack this little business?"

"Sometimes hackers are just having a good time messing with people's computers. They do it for thrills," he responded. "Things are fixed now. I have added some malware to better protect you in the future. I think you will be good to go now."

"Hacked?" I said under my breath. "Ok, thanks, Matt. Your time is appreciated," I said in a more pleasant voice.

"I will check in on you from time to time to see how things are going," he told me.

"Really? Thanks for that. I will sleep better tonight," I told him as he headed out the door.

Matt had left some instructions of things to do and not to do. I had a meeting with the office staff to go over what had happened, how it was fixed, and what to do and not to do going forward. It was a good lesson for all of us.

I really learned two things. First, I needed to keep our systems safe from hackers and protect our confidential information, and second, adopt the IT company's methods of engagement. It was well worth the cost of Matt's visit.

"The locks on the doors are only part of well secured premises," I thought to myself.

Concept # 19

Keep the business safe from intruders of all kinds.

20

Service

It had been a while since I had taken over the business, and I was a lot more comfortable, although not perfect, in my role and duties. The employees, although not perfect, seemed to still have the newness and excitement in their efforts. One idea kept surfacing when we had meetings and discussions regarding our customers. That overriding idea was "What sets us apart from all the competition?" I felt that most of my service techs did not know the answer to this question.

I kept saying, "It's customer service, customer service."

No one seemed to totally grasp that idea; however, and it began to weigh on me. We had to give great service or lose out to the competition.

One of the techs said, "We do our job. We get the stuff fixed and move on."

"Great," I said in response. "That is part of good customer service, but maybe not all."

Another tech told us, "I used to keep track of when each piece of equipment was last serviced, in a log on my phone, and the next time I was at their office, I reminded them that it may be time to service that piece."

"How do they react to the suggestion?" I queried.

He then responded, "Most of them seem to appreciate the suggestion, but rarely will they ask for that service. In some cases they tell me they don't have time and a couple of times they thought I was trying to generate unneeded work."

"So, how do you handle those cases?" I asked.

"Now I just do whatever they want to pay us for. That is it, nothing more," he concluded.

"Any other ways we can give good service to our customers?" I called out, as some of the guys were getting restless with all the talking. No response, just a few shakes of the head.

"Ok, we are about done here. I will come up with some ideas and we can meet in a week or two and talk about it more. If each of you will make a list of ideas you have, I will appreciate it. Have a good day," I finished.

The next time we met, there were no real additional answers. We seemed stumped, but I knew that we had to distinguish ourselves from the rest of the competition or lose out. I really believed it.

One day, about a week later, I remembered the IT guy, Matt, who came in to fix our hacked computers. I remembered his nicely pressed and logoed shirt and the wrap that encircled his little car. This gave me some ideas.

We had a staff meeting later in the week to discuss them. I explained to them what I saw when Matt showed up. How professional he looked and how his car was decorated. Many had seen him and his car. Some liked it and some didn't.

After a discussion, we voted. I say voted, but with or without the vote, I decided we were going to implement these ideas. The majority voted in favor of shirts with the company logo. I told them that we would put nice, tasteful advertising in prominent places on any company vehicles. We would be the envy of our competition. I was sure of it.

Another idea was proposed. Instead of a tech pestering the clients about needed work, we would find some software that would track each client's equipment and factory maintenance programs and send emails to the clients at the prescribed time. It would come from our office and not from the tech. That way, the techs would not be the sales person but the one to carry out the maintenance schedules and not wear thin any goodwill they had built up over the years. I went to a few trade shows and other gatherings and found out that this kind of software increased sales of existing clients. I don't remember the percentage, but the software paid for itself many times over.

One more idea was to offer training classes to any client's workers to teach them how to use all the functionality that each piece of equipment had. We saw many instances where the equipment was not used to its fullest capacity. Many of the bells and whistles were never used or even considered and would probably make a big difference in a diagnosis.

Most in the staff meeting that day thought that that was a very good idea. We could go to the medical office or use our room that we had for training purposes. This idea met with a wave of excitement. It took away the tension that had been there.

We developed a "hot shot" service that allowed rush jobs to be placed ahead of other work in case of certain kinds of emergencies. This allowed for our customers to be able to have something fixed in an expeditious manner, should the need arise. We already had been doing this, but the program needed to be formalized.

We felt that they would add some pride in our service and that the customers would take notice. It could take a while to put this plan in motion, but we all felt that these ideas would be well worth the effort and expense.

Last, I set up a suggestion box in the office for employees to put in suggestions on an anonymous or named basis. The box had suggestions in it regularly.

Concept #20

Give your customers the best service available.

21

Avoiding Stagnation

The one thing I knew I needed to do was to increase total revenue, which some called top line revenue or gross sales. That meant finding new clients and generating additional sales revenue with existing clients. That was my job. I was a pretty good salesman, I thought, and knew how to manage active ongoing accounts. After all, this is one of the main reasons I bought the business, because I saw this gap, this gaping hole in the previous owner's way of running MERI. His sales had been stagnant for several years. He even told me that he did not want to add new business because it would just generate additional risks and other problems. But I knew that more sales, if managed correctly, would add more to the bottom line, the net profit. Actually, it sounded easier than it really it turned out to be.

I had sales experience, my wife was in marketing, and Dan knew something about a lot of things. I felt as if I had the resources to push the business to a higher level. Our new uniforms, logoed trucks, and client tracking system would be a good start, but there was much more to be done. We had some excess capacity and knew where to find additional qualified Techs, when needed.

One evening Dan, his wife Grace, and Lori and I were at the Club having dinner. Grace was a marketing guru and Dan and Grace had been through the drill with their own company, so I decided to pick their brains as the opportunity presented itself.

I started off, "What do you all think about our new logoed shirts and trucks?"

Lori interjected, "I love the logo, seeing how I developed the look."

Grace gave a laugh and nodded her head in agreement.

"Oh, they're Ok, I guess," Dan began. "I think I would have done it a little differently, but they didn't have the wraps when I was in business. It would not have been a good fit with what we were doing anyway."

"I think it is a good beginning, but there has to be more to it than a logo on a shirt and decorated vans," I responded. "Maybe you experts can give me some ideas that I can take and figure out how to implement."

Lori opened up, "I think you need to take the logo and totally redo your website and add as much social media as possible. Make it where your website is in the top five when someone does an internet search. That is where it needs to be. It is called SEO, which is short of Search Engine Optimization. I've done both for some of my clients, and I just might help you, if you get me some of that Crème Brule." She poked me in the ribs with her elbow.

"That's a great idea," Grace piped in.

While we ate the desert, Dan gave some sage advice, "Your business has a great list of established customers. Set a goal to get at least one referral from each client each year. That way you get a warm lead. If you can get twenty percent of the referrals to do business with you, that will be a real nice healthy grow profile."

"I like that. I've tried cold calling, and it is brutal. Necessary in some cases, but brutal, none the less," I commented.

Dan began, "Don't try to sell anything. Try to come in as a consultant and find out what is going on with their equipment. Try to solve whatever problems they might have. Help them resolve their worst headaches. They will love you for it."

"Another great idea," I thought. He was good. I appreciated his input.

"One more thing. To generate leads for sales calls, have your techs write down names and numbers of other offices in the buildings they visit. Maybe have them leave a card or grab a card of the doc who works there. This city has loads of medical offices, and I'll bet you have less than twenty percent of the business," he said.

"Well, it is more like twenty-three percent. Thank you very much," I cracked.

"Twenty or twenty-three, you still have a lot that you can add to your stable of clients," Dan said, defending himself.

"Hey, there are a few other things you can try," Grace added, to soften the tone.

"What do you have, Grace?" I questioned her.

"There are medical magazines that are produced for local readers and are focused on the medical industry. You can run ads in some of them," she stated.

"That is a really good idea," Lori added. "You can also attend various medical networking functions. There are luncheons and evening gatherings and they are cheap compared to full scale advertising. They can be fun too. Just being seen by your customers will add credibility to the business. Maybe even donate to some of their charities. Doctors love that. And don't forget to be active in the Chamber of Commerce and the local chapter of the American Medical Association. Those should pay off as you meet and greet and network. Oh, before I finish, you should develop a marketing plan similar to your business plan but focused on marketing efforts. You know, what to do and how to do it."

"Yes, your advertising needs to be focused on your industry. General advertising will not hit your target prospect, it must be focused," Dan added.

All these are good ideas and hopefully lead to additional sales and happy clients.

"Well, my dessert is gone, and I am getting tired. I need to be up early for a client meeting tomorrow," Lori told us.

"I'm beat, too," Grace added.

I put the check on my account, because I felt like I was the one who got the most benefit from our dinner. It was an inexpensive lesson in advertising.

Concept # 21

Promote the business through consultative selling, advertising, marketing, and social media.

22

Oh, No!

Something was not adding up. My cash reserves were down to almost nothing, and I began to worry. I couldn't figure it out. I looked through our accounting records, talked to the bookkeeper, and whatever else I could think of, but no answers. I was stumped, but still needed to make payroll on Friday. It began to eat at me. I did not let anyone know, except the bookkeeper, who was my alarm in the beginning.

About three one morning, I couldn't sleep. It kept going through it in my mind, over and over again. The Tech's were busy and had been. We had not purchased any fixed assets or spent extra money on much of anything. There was just no cash. My stomach was in knots, but I didn't want to say anything to the employees and get them worried. This was my own little crisis that I needed to solve without sounding the alarm, but I needed help.

That evening, at dinner, Lori and I went through a few things to see if she had any ideas. All that did was to make her squirm. Neither of us liked this situation, but neither had any ideas what to do. Most of our excess cash had been put in as a down payment and her salary was only enough to keep food on the table. It was scary, and I really did not want her to go through this on my account. Things were fine before I had the wild hair to buy this business.

"Maybe it is time to make a draw on our line of credit," I said with worry.

"I thought you were not going to do that except for desperate situation?" she responded.

"This is pretty desperate," I retorted. "I have to make payroll on Friday, and I don't know where the funds are coming from, except from a bank line of credit. There are a few other bills that need attention, too."

"Well, we don't have much, if any, in savings after that big down payment you had to make," she reminded me.

"Why don't you give Dan a call? You haven't seen or spoken to him for a few weeks," she suggested.

"That is a great idea. Thanks for thinking of it," I said with a little hope in my tone. "I heard that he and his buddy are playing golf tomorrow, so maybe I will crash their party."

"OK, I can go for that. Just don't come home with scary news to tell me. My days are hard enough as it is." she instructed.

I got to the Club and was surprised to arrive as Dan was walking up to door. "Hey, what are you doing here?" he asked with surprise. "I thought we were on for later in the week."

"Well, honestly I have a problem that I need help with," I told him.

"Do you have time to walk nine?" he asked. "My golf partner called me just before I drove up to the valet. He said something about his daughter's something or other. I didn't understand what he told me. I really wanted to play today, too."

"My mind is not on golf today. I really only have a few minutes for coffee or something quick. But I really need some advice," I begged.

"OK. Let me go in and cancel our tee time, and I will meet you in the coffee shop," he told me.

His favorite spot was taken, but that was ok. I wanted a little privacy anyway. I wasn't used to spilling my guts in front of strangers.

As he sat down, he said, "What's up?"

"Well, it is my cash flow," I confessed. "It is very thin at the current time, and I've got to make payroll and pay a few suppliers. I went through the books and can't figure it out."

"Let's explore a few things," he said in a consultative manner. "Are sales still normal or better?"

"Yes, sales are even up about ten percent or so," I responded.

"Any major expenses or other cash outlays?" he went on.

"No, just the normal bills and payroll," I told him.

"What is your receivable turnover ratio?" he asked.

"I don't really know. I haven't checked it lately," I confessed.

"One last question. Is your inventory higher or lower than normal?" he inquired.

"There was a deal a few weeks ago. You know, buy so many and get more for a discount. That kind of thing, so I stocked up. But it was only a few thousand," I said defensively.

"Get on the phone and ask your bookkeeper what shape your accounts receivable are in. She will know what to tell you," he said looking at my phone that was stuffed in my shirt pocket.

I called and asked a few questions. Then, Dan and I picked up our forty questions session.

"Well, what'd she tell you? he asked.

"ARs are about twice as high as normal. We even have a couple that are over forty-five days past due. It is a couple of our best customers, and I don't want to make them mad," I told him.

"So, you are willing to come here and ask me to solve your problems, probably stay up all night and then tell your employees that there is no money to pay them, because you don't want to make a doctor angry or rock his boat? Listen, medical offices are notoriously bad business people. If they get short on funds, they will squeeze anyone and everyone they can to keep their cash balances intact. Guaranteed!" he finished abruptly. "Here is my advice, and it is only going to cost you the price of that cup of coffee. Give those two good clients a call or go by and see them and tell you don't work for free. Then, don't let them, or anyone else, ride you like that. Got it?" he asked as he stared right at me.

"Yes, sir," I responded, feeling like a school boy.

"And one more thing. The next time you want to fill your shelves with parts that will take months to use, just say no thanks. There is a time value to money, and space on your shelves is not free, either. Keep your cash. Know where it should be and stick as close to that number as possible. Remember your cash flow projections?" he asked. I nodded.

"Those projections were done for this very reason. The bank surely wanted them and you should use them and stick to it as closely as you can. Now, once cash builds up, then you might, just might, begin to think about spending money on extra inventory and allowing you best clients to ride you. But not until then. Does all that make sense?" he questioned me at the end of his scolding.

I sheepishly nodded. I should have known. I should have been able to figure all this out. I felt, well let's just say, it wasn't my best work.

After my dressing down, I went straight to the office and had the bookkeeper call the two delinquent doctors.

"Oh, did we forget to pay that? Sorry we will mail it today," was what I heard from the noise I could hear coming out of the phone.

"No. I will go drive over there and pick up a check and take it straight to the bank," I told her. "I don't want to lose another night's sleep. See you later this afternoon."

Concept #22

Manage your inventory and your accounts receivable closely.

23

Stubs

Having figured that out, and escaping a near disaster, and seeing my cash recovering, I began to think about something Dan had told me sometime before I ever bought the business. "Cash is king," he told me over and over again. I think I was beginning to understand what he was telling me. It was an extremely sickening feeling to think that I had gotten so close to missing payroll. How could I have been so stupid to even have to consider such a thing? Many people depended on their pay checks and frankly deserved them, and probably more. I felt really grateful for the advice I had gotten and that things worked out well. What a relief! In the long run, it was a very cheap cup of coffee.

Lori and I had been having some remodeling done on our home. I was talking to the contractor and asked him how he handled his cash flow. It was a very interesting conversation. His name was Stubs. He had lost one of his fingers in a work accident and had a middle stub instead of a full finger.

Stubs began his little story. "Once, when I was younger and new to the business, I landed a large, very large remodel. It paid fifty percent up front and forty-five percent upon completion and the balance after a ten day hold back period for punch list items. So, when we signed the contract, and I got the first payment of fifty percent, I felt like I was rich. I mean, loaded with cash in my bank account and to spare. It felt real good."

"I could imagine," I responded.

"Anyway, about the same time one of my buddies wanted to sell his ski boat. It was nice and had all the add-ons you could imagine. I figured since I had some cash in the bank, I could put a big chunk down and make the payments smaller. My wife was not in favor of the idea, but the gleam of the boat's exterior and the sound of the roaring motor won out. I made the deal," he said, continuing his story.

"Did it pull you up quickly?" I asked.

"Wow, it was unbelievable. It was everything I had ever hoped for. But then it happened," he continued.

"What happened?" I asked, with some anticipation.

"Well, I started the job. Before long I had no money to buy some needed materials and pay the subs," he said.

"Go on," I urged.

"Stupid me, I had spent the money for the job on a stinking boat! What an idiot I was!" he exclaimed.

"The down payment on the boat should have been saved and used to get the job farther down the road."

"What did you do?"

"Fortunately, my banker was understanding and had had a good experience with my other loans, so he was able to refinance the boat, allowing me time to sell the thing and replenish my cash position. He also granted me a small, very small revolving line of credit. He was a life saver. I owe him big time," Stubs told me.

In my mind I could hear Dan telling me, "Cash is king. Take care of your cash." His words played in my mind over and over again. Another thing he said was something like this: "Cash flow is not profit. Cash flow is the movement of cash through the business. Profit is what is left after all the bills are paid. Never confuse the two."

I went back to my cash flow projections and reworked them with the new information and understanding I had. I determined that day to have cash flow projections done on a quarterly basis, review them on a monthly basis, and make changes as needed. I had felt the empty feelings and did not like them. I did not want to feel them ever again.

I believe I now know what is meant by "free cash." It is cash that is available to spend. Cash that is not set aside for a specific item, such as payroll or material purchases. I wanted to be sure I knew what bills were due on what day. I wanted to have a solid estimate of my incoming and outgoing cash—my cash flow position statement. It is now a must have.

Concept #23

Cash is King! Don't confuse cash flow and profit.

24

Peter Somebody

All this made my mind swim. I needed to figure out how to handle the business end of the business. I needed to plan better, manage cash better, and all the rest.

Over the years as I listened to the stock reports, it always seemed like the current quarter or the next quarter was the most important. I just don't see how they can do it. I felt like I needed a longer term approach, and at least, look at the business from an annual perspective and even over a three- to five-year horizon. Quarterly was much too often, and I was just one guy trying to get it all done. Besides, I did not have to report to stockholders, just my wife and the employees and customers. Maybe this line of thought should have been done in the beginning, before I bought the business, but at the time all that I could do was to think about the things on my to-do list in order to close on the purchase.

Anyway, I began to research business strategy and business planning on the internet. I came across an article that quoted a guy named Peter something. I should have written it down, but oh well, it is still on the internet. This Peter was a leadership consultant and executive coach. He seemed to know what he was talking about. He said something like this: "Strategic planning is important, but execution is imperative. You must develop a rhythm of execution."

By this, I think he meant that once you have established your strategic plan and set the goals to attain your plan, you should spend time on a regular basis working to execute the plan. Weekly is a bit much for most, but certainly monthly is doable. Peter stated in the article "at a minimum, quarterly is essential. If you don't do it, no one else will. It is your business and no one else's."

The article explained, "Strategic planning is more of an intermediate or long term look at the future and where you want to take your business. Goal setting is where you develop the steps to reach your strategic plan.

Setting goals breaks down the long term into shorter term baby steps. You know the old saying, that to eat an elephant you must take one bite at a time. Well, that is goal setting. It is working on your strategic plan, one bite at a time."

It made sense to me. I had goals but did not review them often. Most of the time I was flying by the seat of my pants, to put it mildly. I determined to begin to use this method on a regular basis and try to work on my business from time to time and not just work in the business. Here are some of the things that I mean by working on the business. All of these items can be worked into a strategic plan and have goals set around them.

- Get the business into a positon that it will run itself so that I do not have to be there all the time
- Decide if it makes sense to expand the business into different territories
- Find out if there are similar businesses for sale in my market or in other markets to help expand mine
- Determine the intended outcome of the business, and position the future toward that end
- Decide how far I want to take it
- Decide if I want to make it into a franchise type of business and create franchises in other markets?
- Determine if there larger companies in the same business that may want to buy my business from me in the future; if so, position the business toward that outcome.
- Find out which other products and services can be developed to augment the business and make it better.

These are questions I asked myself and had long discussions with Dan and Lori about over an extended period of time. The questions and the contemplation of the answers to those questions, took a lot of effort. I worked to determine them and make decisions about the answers. In fact, I have not totally found satisfactory answers to all of these questions, but I do spend time on a regular basis considering each. It is a puzzle that can be solved, and I am going to solve it one of these days.

Concept #24

Develop a business strategy.

Keep in mind the difference between the long and the short term.

25

Just in Case

Life as a business owner was not as easy and carefree as I had imagined. I didn't have a boss; I had many bosses, my employees, suppliers, and customers. It was a lot to manage and keep on top of; a big job indeed!

My one respite from it all was the now weekly golf date with Dan. It was something I could look forward to. It gave me time to think, get my head straight, and gain advice from my good friend and mentor, Dan.

The best time to straighten things out in my mind was when we walked the Executive course. The gentle hypnotic sound of the clubs hitting each other as I walked put me into a different state of mind and helped me think through various issues. It was a much needed break from my normal daily routine, a chance to get it right, whatever "it" was.

Today the weather was near perfect, and I was feeling good and making some great shots. About the third hole, I began to think about some of the what-if's. What if we had a fire or one of my Techs did not do his job properly and the machine would not give a proper reading or if I had a heart attack or any other tragic thing you could think of. I had the basic insurance coverage required by the bank, but I really had not been through any unexpected difficulty to understand how the insurance worked or even if it would cover the costs of losses and all the rest of the possibilities. It began to take over my thinking and my golf game.

My shots began to drift left or right and my putts didn't quite make their targets. I didn't like what I was thinking or feeling, so I began to pick at Dan's brain.

"Ok, what happens when things go wrong? You know, in the business," I questioned.

"What do you mean by wrong?" he asked.

"What if a tech was in an auto accident while driving one of my trucks or we had a fire and it destroyed all or part of our building? Well, you know, that kind of wrong," I told him.

"Don't be so paranoid," he barked at me. "You are no good as a worry wart."

"But those thing can and do happen all the time," I said earnestly.

"That's right, they do happen but they are manageable and that is why you have insurance," he instructed. "You do have insurance, don't you?"

"Of course I do. The bank required me to carry enough to cover their loan amounts," I responded.

Dan looked at me and said, "I sure hope you have more than just the bare minimum."

"Well, what do you think I should have and how much?" I asked in a somewhat confused tone.

"You need to have enough coverage to replace the assets needed to keep the business going. And there are varying other types of coverage that you should seriously consider buying," he said.

"Ok, I am all ears. Lay it on me," I prodded.

Dan began, "There are many kinds of insurance, like liability and E & O or Errors and Omissions, malpractice, business interruption, just to name a few of the more important coverages."

"I guess I am not an insurance expert, so will you explain them to me?" I asked meekly.

"Let's hit our tee shots, and I will begin as we walk toward the balls," he suggested.

My shot went about two thirds of its normal distance because I was still worrying about insurance. Dan hit the ball, and boy, did he crush it.

"Now that was a nice shot," I said.

"Thanks, now for insurance. Errors and omissions (E&O) and malpractice are similar and are there just in case one of the machines you repair is not calibrated correctly and gives a false reading and a doctor makes a wrong diagnosis for a patient. If the patient gets the wrong drug or other recommendation from the doc and things don't go well, it could come back to you to pay for whatever damage might be incurred."

"Well, that sounds pretty scary. I might talk to my insurance agent about that one," I replied.

"Of course, there is liability coverage in case of a truck wreck or if someone is hurt at your office, and one last one to check out is business interruption coverage, which will pay you a certain percentage to cover ongoing expenses if for some reason you cannot conduct business as normal. Things like a fire in the building or a bad storm that shuts down your repair shop. You have to be very careful and understand what it covers and also what is not covered. And one last thing, be sure you have workman's comp to cover hurt workers," Dan concluded.

"That's it. First thing in the morning I will set up a meeting with my insurance agent to go through all of these options. Thanks for the advice. Now, will you please hit the ball?" I wisecracked.

Standing on the next tee box, I had always loved the view toward the west. The tee box was one of the highest spots on the course, and you could see for miles. It was a fabulous view, to say the least. We both stood there gazing out at the panoramic view.

Dan broke the silence. "Here are a couple of more things to discuss with your agent," he said calmly.

"Go for it," I directed.

"Fraud, you need to be sure that no one in your company commits fraud and that no one, suppliers or customers or whomever, commits fraud against you. There is insurance to cover that, but if you have the correct procedures in place, it will take care of the most prevalent. Fraud, either external or internal, can shut you down. It has happened all too often," Dan warned.

"You're scaring me now. Anything else before I have that heart attack we just spoke about?" I asked with fear.

"Well, actually, yes, there is one more thing that needs to be dealt with," Dan said.

"OK, quick while I can still stand," I urged him.

"It is important to find out what governmental regulations there might be regarding your service business. There may be none, but you really need to find out for sure if there are rules and regulations that need to be followed. If so, you need to follow them exactly so you do not have other issues popping up that have to be handled, that will only take a lot of time and money to fix. Governmental agencies can hand out large fines and jail time if an infraction is serious enough."

"You're killing me here, Dan. I need to find four or five kinds of insurance, develop a procedure manual to be sure everyone does his or her job correctly. I need to find out if the government wants to meddle in my business. Is that all?" I asked defensively.

"Sure. That is enough to think about for now. I'm sure we will come up with more, maybe next week. What do you say?" Dan joked in a nicer, softer tone, trying to ease some of my angst.

"Whatever!"

Concept # 25

Keep the business safe from fraud, external liability, and be compliant with governmental regulation.

26

Saving Twenty-five Cents

It had been a few years since I bought MERI. We had done rather well. Sales had almost quadrupled, while staff and other expenses had increased just about double, leaving a nice profit margin at the end of each year. The problem I faced was taxes. After all was said and done, I had to pay extra for the last several years. I hated the whole idea of taxes.

I thought of everything I could think of to get out of paying so much to the IRS. We established a profit sharing plan to help the employees, in addition to matching their retirement contributions up to four percent. We had a great medical insurance plan that the employees loved, matched their Social Security payments, and anything else that was legal. We still had to pay. "That's no fun," I thought to myself.

Lori and I had saved back more than our original down payment to buy the business and had almost paid off our house, not to mention the loan to purchase MERI. Lori thought about quitting her work, but she felt she would get bored. We were not able to have children so we did not have to face expenses related to raising children. She and I lived simply. Our cars were older models and both paid for. We took smaller vacations, which were not overly expensive. We were doing just fine, except we had to pay taxes every year, loads of them.

One day, toward the end of the year, I scheduled a short meeting with the CPA, who was part of our Advisory Board. We did not have our financial statements audited, so he felt comfortable on the Board and giving advice.

We met at his office and the first thing he said was, "Just hope you have to pay a million dollars in taxes."

I blurted out, "What, are you crazy?"

"No. The more money you make the more taxes you will have to pay. It is a fact of business life."

"Wow, maybe I should stop working so hard?" I said halfheartedly.

"Now, don't get too excited just yet. We have a lot to discuss," he commented, trying to settle me down a little. "Just remember, you don't want to spend a dollar to save twenty-five cents in taxes." .

"OK, OK, what ideas do you have?" I asked more calmly.

"First of all, we never want to evade taxes, just so we can say we didn't pay them. There is a big difference in tax avoidance and tax evasion. One is legal and one will put you in jail. Not a real fun place to be, either," he quipped.

"I would never suggest any kind of evasion. I am looking for legitimate ideas to cut Uncle Sam's take. Just a little," I told him. "Give me a list of things we can do, or at least consider, to cut our tax bill."

"OK, here are some ideas that we can discuss one by one," he began. "The first thing I think you might consider is to build your own building. I am sure you qualify for a loan and your monthly payment shouldn't go up much at all. And all of the interest is tax deductible."

"My own building, huh? Now, that is an idea, but how will it save taxes?" I questioned.

"It is more of a long-term view. In addition to the interest deduction, tax savings can come when you customize the office space and fit the work area with nice work tables and storage bins. You can also build a larger space now and grow into it down the road," he told me.

"What else?" I asked.

"Retirement. You can increase your retirement savings to meet the maximum levels allowed by law. I do believe you have some extra you can and should contribute," he said, looking at me to try and read my face. "Here are some other minor things you can do. Give to charity, give away your old equipment and not sell it. Pay some expenses this year for next year's work. This can catch up with you, however. Charge off any and all accounts that may be way past due. If they are ever paid, you will have to recapture those losses, which will increase your profit and thus your taxes."

"Anything else?" I asked.

"Sure, there lots of things to buy and spend money on, but you are still spending money buying those things or paying taxes. Remember, don't spent a dollar to save twenty-five cents in taxes," he repeated.

"I know, I know." I muttered. "I am just curious, however. What are some ways different people use to evade taxes?" I asked sheepishly.

"You mean you haven't figured that out yet?" he questioned.

"No, I try to be honest," I told him.

He began, "Some business keep two sets of accounting records. One real one and one designed to show the IRS if needed. I think it is too much work for such a large exposure. Some companies will just not report income or do barter deals or take cash and not report it as sales."

"I've heard of some of those," I responded.

"A few others are counting personal expenses as business expenses when they are not legitimate. And just plain falsifying some of the internal records. This is a bit tricky when you have an honest bookkeeper, which you want to have for sure. You have to lie to them as well as yourself in order to pull off some of the deception. I would not want to have to hide anything from anyone. It is too hard to keep all the lies straight in one's mind. I don't understand how people can do that. One last thing, if you ever did any of this and I find out about it, and I would sooner or later, I might have to turn you in to the authorities myself," he told me candidly.

"I appreciate that. I would not want to put you in that position or have you part of anything like all that stuff," I promised him.

"Before we wrap up our discussion, let's begin to outline a possible new building and augmenting your retirement," he suggested.

"Sure, I have some time. Let's begin," I said with a smile. "Thanks for the advice."

Concept #26

Explore all legitimate approaches to reduce the tax burden.

SELLING YOUR BUSINESS

27

Transitioning

For the past several years I had business brokers call me from time to time and try to get me to list MERI for sale with their firms. I always said, "No thanks." End of story, maybe, but not always. The calls made me contemplate how much the thing was worth. What would I do if I sold it? Would it get me enough money to live out my life in a manner that we had become used to living? These and other questions went through my mind when I received those phone calls.

I spoke to my Board of Advisors, my attorney, the CPA, my financial planner, and on and on. But no satisfaction.

One day, however, a broker had called. The very next day was a golf date with Dan. I figured, "I might as well get his opinion. I've gotten everyone else's take on selling." I decided to make that the topic of our match the next day. The weather looked as if a good day was lining up for us.

As usual, we met in the Club House to check in for our tee time. Our scheduled tee off time was 9:05. I arrived a little early, so decided to hit a few balls on the practice range. Dan was already there with his bucket almost gone.

"What time did you show up?" I asked.

"Oh, you know, just a while ago," he said cunningly. I knew he was out for blood today.

"I'm sure. You must have gotten a half full bucket of balls too," I said.

"I hope you are on your game today," he challenged.

"I was born ready," I shot back.

"Looks like it's going to be a good one today," he said, as he bent over to put the next ball on the tee.

I waited just a few seconds and in his back swing, I said, "Yes, a real good one."

He stopped the forward motion of his swing and glared at me. "You trying to get in my head already?" he questioned.

"No, no, go ahead. Sorry to talk during your swing," I said in a cagey tone.

About that time, we heard our names called out over the loud speaker.

"Time to go," I said, packing up my clubs for the ride to the first tee box.

The morning was bright, and the sun was directly in our eyes for our first shot.

"Can you help me watch the ball?" Dan asked, setting up for the drive.

"I will if you watch mine. Go for it," I responded. "Holy cow, you hit that one out of the park."

"It felt good," he told me.

"I think it is time for me to hit one out of the park too, and I don't mean the golf ball," I stated.

"What then?" he asked.

"I think I am about ready to sell MERI and I need to hit a good one," I told him.

"What!" he exclaimed.

"Sure, it may be time," I told him.

"Are you ready to sell?" he asked.

"I've never sold before, so I'm not sure. Maybe you can coach me in my golf game today and selling my business," I said.

"We will have some time today. The foursome ahead of us seem slow. It might be fun to discuss," he told me.

"Great. Where will we begin?" I asked.

"Let me list a few things to think about and then we can discuss each as we go. That works, doesn't it?"

"It sounds good to me. What's first?" I asked.

Dan began a little explanation of things he had to do when he sold his business. "First of all you have to get your mind ready to sell."

"What does that mean?" I questioned.

"You need to think about what you will do going forward, how your employees will handle things and how to transition to a new owner and life style for yourself," Dan told me.

"Well, that is a lot to think on, but I have thought about those things already. I am satisfied that it is time to sell and have some ideas of what to do with my time, once the sale closes," I told him. "As for the employees, it will depend on who I sell to and what they are looking for, but I do have them in mind. After all, we have grown close over the years. Last, Lori and I have talked about what I, or we, will do at that time. We do have a few ideas."

"That is a start. Now you must think about valuing the business. You only get to sell it once, and you need to get the most you can."

"That's for sure," I interrupted.

Dan continued, "Then you must think about being sure everything is looking its best. Things like your accounting records, accounts receivable, and being sure all of the equipment is in top shape."

"What else?" I asked.

"Taxes will have to be paid on your profit, you have to find a qualified buyer. Think about using a broker to guide you and help negotiate the sale and the role you will play in the transition period when a buyer takes possession of the day-to-day chores."

"There really is a lot to work on," I responded, surprised.

Dan said, "I suggest you get online and read as much as you can to find out all of the little nuisances related to selling."

"I've done a little research, but I need to spend a lot more time looking at as much as possible," I told him.

"I think those guys are far enough down the fairway that you can hit your next shot," he told me.

I had a nice drive but, again, he out drove me on that hole. He always seemed to out-drive me by twenty-five yards or more. It was discouraging sometimes. I set up for my shot and heard him bellow, "Nope, they are still down in that little valley. I can see the top of their cart. Relax for a few minutes."

"Thanks. I did not see them. I probably can't hit it that far anyway, but we have time. Maybe we can finish up your tutorial," I suggested.

"That is pretty much all I have to offer. Maybe just prioritize those items in a logical order and work on them one by one to get everything lined up properly. You know what they say, 'to eat an elephant, just take one bite at a time.'"

"Yes, that is an oldie," I thought.

Concept # 27

There is a lot to consider when it is time to sell.

28

How Much?

A day or two after the long golf course discussion with Dan, I had an almost equally long discussion with Lori. We together decided that it was time to sell MERI. It felt good. I was confident that we could get a good price for the business and that the sale would go a long way toward reaching some of our personal financial goals, but we had to do it right, because there are no "do overs", no "king's x's." or anything of that sort.

The first thing was for us to come up with a number that made sense for us and that would make sense to a prospective buyer of the business. I decided to spend a decent amount of time finding the right number and asked help from a good friend of mine, who knew one of the best business brokers in town.

One afternoon, I met Celeste at a local coffee shop. After trading pleasantries and her selling me on her expertise, Celeste said, "OK, tell me what your goals are regarding selling your business. You know, things like, trying to keep current employees, keeping the name of the business intact, the current level of customer satisfaction, and those kinds of things. This way I can focus on the things most important to you and not waste a lot of time discussing items you really have no interest in."

"That sounds like a good place to start," I responded.

I gave her what I felt was the necessary feedback as she nodded her head from time to time and seemed to listen with good intent.

Then I broke from her line of questioning. "What I really need to do is to come up with a sales price that will be good for me and make sense to a buyer."

"That is what everyone wants, and we are getting there," she told me. She asked more questions, took notes, and tried to redirect the conversation in her direction.

I felt as if they were valid questions, but I wanted to get down to the nitty gritty. "What is my business worth?" I thought to myself with a bit of frustration.

I think she sensed my anxiety, and we began to go over a few items that could get us to a number.

She began to get down to some of the things I needed. "There are a number of ways to value your business," she explained.

"OK, I'm listening," I told her.

"Market value is the best, but if there are no similar businesses in your area or even in the state, it can be difficult to figure it out."

"Well, I was glad that she didn't say something like what a willing buyer and seller agree upon. That would have put a quick end to the discussion," I thought.

She went on, "If we can find one or more similar sells, then we need to adjust the price for things like profitability, cash on hand, owner's special expenses, or pet projects the owner may have been working on. Oh, yes, we would need to add back the owner's pay and other compensation. This number will change with new owners and different ways of accounting, etc."

"What about things like cash flow and net present value and the value of the tangible assets?" I asked.

"Those items do come into play, and you can use them to figure out a value, but those items can vary depending on how they are figured. Different people have different definitions for many financial terms," she responded. "A couple of other methods can be a pure asset sale or a value based on profitability. An assets sale takes into consideration the actually value of equipment, inventory, accounts receivable and all other assets. This method can be subject to a lot of negotiation back and forth."

"Yes, I can see that. I argue with my CPA over the value of things to depreciate. It can be a constant battle," I said.

"The last method I mentioned is based on profit before tax. Some call it "Net Present Value." Basically, you take profit and add back things that may be one-time expenses or special projects and divide that number by an anticipated percent return, like say nine percent. So if you had average adjusted before tax profit of say, one hundred thousand consistently each year or at least for the past several years and divide that by nine percent you get a value of just over one point one million dollars. In other words, if you had the one point one million and wanted a nine percent return, this would give you the one hundred thousand," she said, taking a breath.

"Oh, one more method in some industries is they multiply the adjusted before-tax profit by one, two, three, or four, maybe more depending on the industry. So in the example I just told you, if the multiple is four then the business is worth four hundred K. You say, 'why the difference'? It is really based on industry norms, and it does vary. These can be more of a benchmark and not a true value. So there is some research to be done to come up with the right number," she said.

"What is the norm in the medical equipment industry?" I asked.

"I do not know, but when you sign my listing agreement, then I will begin to do the research," she said, handing me a contract form to look at. I am sure she hoped I would sign it on the spot.

"Well, let me read over the agreement and get back to you," I replied. "Oh, by the way, what are normal fees for your services?"

"No fee," she said. "We usually receive a ten percent commission once the sale is closed and funded."

"Well, that could be a lofty amount," I thought.

"All right, then. I will read this form and give you a call. Will that work?" I asked her.

"I guess so. I do have a few other businesses coming on, which may cause me to be overloaded. But, whatever works for you," she answered.

"I'll take my chances on that. I have a lot to think about right now," I said.

"I understand, no hurry, really," she said in a softer tone. "One last thing, you can value your business however you think is right and whatever you can get someone to buy it for. There are many different methods."

I thought to myself with a smile on my face. "OK, she said it." It was the trite old saying of whatever a willing buyer and seller agree to. I was done with this meeting and probably her, too.

"Ten percent, my foot!" I thought as I walked out of the building.

Concept #28

Spend time determining the right price, before you go to market.

29

Watch Out!

A few days after my discussion with Celeste and spending loads of time researching on the internet and talking to owners of similar business, I decided to give Dan a chance to shower me, once again, with his knowledge and experience, on the golf course. I needed a nice get-away as business pressures had been mounting, mostly related to the sale of MERI. Selling made me a little nervous. What if it didn't sell? Or I sold it too cheap? Playing the "what if" game was not a good thing, especially right now.

I heard a story of a guy who called a business owner, unsolicited, and tried to buy his business. After lots of meetings and questions and all the rest over an extended period of time, they guy wanted to "steal" the business for the price of the assets. After the owner had let down his guard and began to dream about sitting on a beach somewhere with a cool drink in his hand, and was all primed to sell, the bomb shell was dropped. The story went on and said the guy tried to hoodwink the owner into selling the business for a ridiculous price. That story, sobering as it was, got me to thinking a lot, to say the least.

The next morning was splendid. The weather almost perfect for us, I had gotten a good night's sleep. Dan seemed to be in a good mood, to boot. We headed out for the nine-hole executive course. I was a little worried that we would not have enough time to cover all of my questions. I needed to understand what I was in for when it came to negotiating the sales of MERI. But wouldn't you know it, two of the oldest members were ahead of us, and they were also walking. I now knew I would have enough time to get all my questions answered.

About the second hole, Dan began, "Ok, what's on your mind today?"

"I'm glad you asked," I responded. "I have a couple of potential offers on my business, and I need to know what might be in store for me during this process. I want to be ready for whatever."

"Tell me about your potential offers and I will see what I can come up with. This will be interesting. Thanks for trusting me on this one," he offered.

"My first idea is not original to me, but it makes loads of sense. Price may not be the most important thing when selling your business. It is important, but there are many factors that need to be considered."

"Really? I thought price was the ultimate thing. The more I get, the more I have for retirement. Right?" I asked.

"Well, in theory that is correct, but you need to consider when you get the money, all up front or over time. This can make a huge difference in taxes you will owe to Uncle Sam," Dan said. "You also need to have a minimum number in mind that you will accept. Remember you only get one shot at selling. Remember our conversation a few weeks ago?" he reminded me of one of his favorite sayings.

"Is it my turn or yours to tee off?" I asked Dan.

"It is me all the way," he said, pounding his chest.

"I sure wish we had gotten out here a little earlier," Dan told me. "We'd be on the third hole by now."

"Yep, I'm right there with you," I responded.

Just then, we saw one of the guys ahead of us wandering off into the weeds. He must have been looking for a ball.

"What the heck. I can't hit it yet," Dan said, with some irritation in his voice.

"While we have a few minutes, tell me more that I will need to know," I said.

"You, for sure, need to know the buyer and get as much background on them as you can. You need to be assured they are serious with the ability to make the sale happen."

"For sure!" I agreed. "Sort of like that story I read the other day. It was about this guy who almost got what they call hoodwinked or cheated when he tried to sell his business."

"Hoodwinked, I like that word. It is rather descriptive. My dad used to use it when I was a boy," Dan said.

He kept going, "Sometimes, almost always, buyers will come in with a low ball offer, just to test the waters. Don't get offended or take the offer. It is something most try, no matter what. Remember that some will come in too low, but you may find someone willing to pay too much. This can be a bad thing because it may drive them out of business. If you have chosen to finance some or all of the purchase price, then you will have to go through a foreclosure process and the whole thing can spin out of control. Not too high and not too low. Sort of like the story of *The Three Bears*."

"That is one of the funniest things you've said in a while, but don't give up your day job, if you had one," I joked.

"Also, I know you have done this, but be sure everything is in the best order you can make it, the accounting, the facilities, the equipment, etc. This will let a buyer know that you have taken care of things over time. It is important," he preached.

"I know, I know. You have drilled that into my head enough," I responded. "What else?"

"How about, let's play golf and stop talking. The guys behind us are already too close."

It was about the sixth hole. We began our discussion mostly where we left off.

Dan began again, "When you negotiate the sale, you can use things like interest rate on a loan carry back and certain covenants in the agreement to get closer to where the overall price makes sense. If you finance part or all of the sale, which you probably will, be sure to have the ability to look at their accounting records and whatever info you need to, so you will know they are on track and to be able to meet their loan payments and all other obligations. And last, don't be an open book. Keep as much close to your chest as you can, as long as you can. Use each piece of information as another bargaining chip. You know, for the give and take process that will surely come."

We traded comments along with some good shots and a few bad ones as we finished up the round.

"Wow, that took over two and one-half hours. Those guys really slowed us down," I commented.

"Maybe it was all of your questions," Dan said snidely.

"Whatever," I snarled.

Concept # 29

Negotiating the sale of a business can be an art form.

30

Thirty Pounds

It had been a while since I sold MERI. One afternoon I was swimming laps at the Club trying to lose the thirty or so pounds I gained over the past several years. Like the rhythmic clinking of the clubs as I walked down the fairway, my breathing, especially exhaling between strokes, began to mesmerize my mind. The feel of the cool water coursing across the hair on my legs felt good, but pushing my gut through the water was laborious. Why hadn't I taken better care of myself while I was self-employed? Why did I let my body begin to look like the famous doughboy? It was really a shame, too. I already had the membership, paid the monthly dues, but took no time to exercise, sweat, and take care of myself a little better. Frankly, it was rather foolish to do so poorly in that part of my life. I'm sure my psyche and overall demeanor would have been better all-around had I taken care of my physical self. I would have looked and felt better and maybe even felt more confident. I know Lori would have appreciated a better looking husband. My gut was embarrassingly large. Dan even called it "the mound" one day when we were playing a round.

I began to review what I had learned during the years as a business owner and even some of the things I did not learn, like physical exercise. Walking and playing golf was good and burned calories, but did very little for my cardio profile. I had a check-up with the doc. He was pretty hard on me about what bad shape I was in, with borderline high blood pressure and cholesterol. It was not a good report.

Concept # 30

It is as important to take care of your physical health as it is to take care of

your business's health.

Conclusion

All Over Again

That same evening after beating myself up over my poor physical fitness, I began to reflect on the many good things I did learn. I made a mental list as I swam, but then when I finished up the workout, I wrote the list so I could always remember. This is what I learned:

START OR BUY YOUR BUSINESS

1. Think long and hard about the what, where, why, how, and when to start a business.
2. Be very careful not to destroy family ties along the way.
3. Running your own business may be very trying on your emotions and the emotions of those around you.
4. You need to have a plan if things go wrong and the business fails.
5. Decide how to begin your business. (Should you buy an existing business, start from scratch, or buy a franchise?)
6. Spend time determining what kind of legal structure works best for you and the business.
7. Sooner or later you have to decide to decide.
8. Find alternatives, weigh the options carefully, and make a decision.
9. It takes more than just a wish list and an internet search. You must decide what to do and how.
10. The work begins in earnest after coming to a decision.
11. A business plan is a must. Get the ideas out of your head and onto paper
12. Put a team of advisors together. You will need the help.
13. A good and complete loan package and business plan is a must in order to obtain a loan or funds from almost any kind of investor.

RUNNING YOUR BUSINESS

14. Manage your cash closely. Collect your accounts receivable. Keep the right amount of inventory.
15. You need employees you can trust. Then, let them do their work and succeed.
16. Develop a dashboard to help you manage the business day to day.
17. Know the Business from A to Z. It is your life blood.
18. Take good care of your employees.
19. Keep the business safe from intruders of all kinds.
20. Give your customers the best service available.
21. Promote the business through consultative selling, advertising, marketing, and social media.
22. Manage your inventory and your accounts receivable closely.
23. Cash is King! Don't confuse cash flow and profit.
24. Develop a business strategy. Keep in mind the difference between long term and the short term.
25. Keep the business safe from fraud, external liability, and compliant with governmental regulation.
26. Explore all legitimate approaches to reduce the tax burden.

SELLING YOUR BUSINESS

27. There is a lot to consider when it is time to sell.
28. Spend time determining the right price, before you go to market.
29. Negotiating the sale of a business can be an art form.
30. It is as important to take care of your physical health as it is to take care of your business.

I gleaned many treasured nuggets along the way. I made my share of mistakes. Everything I tried did not work, but many things did work. In the end, the score was in favor of things that worked over things that did not work. I honestly feel like it was an overall big win for me, my family, the employees, clients, and suppliers. Some have called this group "stakeholders," those who have a stake in the business, whatever size the stake may be. I think it is a fitting name for all involved.

Lori was still working, so I tried to figure out what was next for me. I didn't want to play golf every day. Once, maybe twice each week was enough. Now this was my focus, to determine what is next in my life. I often had thoughts like, "If I could quit, then I would . . . (fill in the blank)." It changed from time to time, but there was always some little wish or dream out there in the future. I had more time to think about it and come up with a plan. Lori was emphatic about it, too.

Swimming occupied a few hours each week. It was fun to hang out at the club and visit friends, but "there has to be more, something meaningful," I thought.

One day I was at the pool just finishing up my workout, and a younger guy approached me. I had seen him around the club, but mostly at the pool swimming laps. He asked if I would give him a few pointers about a couple of his strokes. I had time, so I obliged him. After that, we saw each other at the pool frequently. I gave him a few ideas to improve his workouts. I wasn't an expert, but had been swimming most of my life, off and on, so I knew enough to give him pointers.

After a month or two of getting to know each other and learning about the other's working life, he wanted me to coach him in the art of starting and running a business. It surprised me because I did not feel like I had any special expertise to teach someone else. Surely, I was no Dan Griffin. Then I thought about the list of concepts that I had learned along the way and agreed to do a little business coaching for him. My terms were that we had to meet at the pool and talk through things before and after our workouts. This would keep both of us coming for a swim. I needed all the encouragement for exercise I could get. I remembered my list of concepts that I written down and figured that would be a good place to begin.

We met the very next week. It started all over again, just like Dan and me on the golf course. It feels good to pass it on. Only time will tell if I help him or not. I wonder what the results will be?

CASE CLOSED

Epilogue
Time to Begin - Go Out and Do It

Well, you have read the book and have all the answers, right? Maybe not. It is just the beginning to a lot of questions to be asked and answered. If you have started to explore the various concepts contained in the book, you are either scared away (which is OK) or you just wanted to get through the book before you begin. Either way, it will work.

There is much research to do and believe me, the internet has more than you can retain. Go there for business plans, spreadsheets, cash flow projection examples, Articles of Incorporation, information about legal advice, businesses for sale, franchises for sale, loan package examples, computer software aids, business brokers and much-much more. It will only cost you your time and effort.

If you have had this little itch for some time, maybe now is the time to scratch it, to put your thoughts and aspirations on paper and move forward. You are not getting younger and it won't be any easier later.

Good luck!

Appendix I
Recurring Revenue Streams

Most businesses these days are developing recurring revenue. If they do not already receive recurring revenue, they will try to figure out a way to develop this source of funds. It is a simple principle. You structure your product and or service in a manner to where you receive regular payments from the customer. Some examples are utility companies such as internet, gas, phone electric, water, etc. Others are insurance companies and mortgage loans. Many gaming and software providers offer access to their product via monthly-payments. Many will take it annually, but it is monthly that they prefer. A monthly payment stream is something that is steady, something that can be counted on month-in and month-out. It makes budgeting easier and more predictable for the company that collects their revenue in this manner.

One other note; recurring revenue usually makes the customers' payments lower and more affordable, which allows them to continue with whatever service they are using. A customer may say, "Well, it's only ten dollars a month. I can afford that." Recurring revenue streams seem like a win-win for all. The company can count on a monthly check and the customer can make easy payments.

The example in this book, MERI, had ongoing service contracts with its customers for extended warranties in case something happened to a piece of their equipment, that was covered under the warranty. In this case, it helped to retain customers and developed a certain loyalty to MERI, and provided MERI with regular funds flow.

Appendix II

"The Multiplier Effect"

The actual title is an Economics 101 term on how the money supply grows. In my definition it is how you can make your business grow more rapidly. This is a concept not often discussed, but it is utilized in many businesses. This is getting away from a "mom and pop" style of business and growing the business into a self-sustaining firm.

Here is an example; let's say I bill out my services for $100 per hour. If I work 40 billable hours per week the most I can make in a week is $4,000. My income is capped. The only way for me to make more money is to work more hours. If I have an off week and do not bill 40 hours, my income will be reduced by $100 for each hour not billed. It is a simple concept.

If I invoke the "multiplier effect", I find others who are competent in the business and have them work for me as an employee. To follow on the example above, I hire 4 others to work for me and they are billed at $100 per hour. (This assumes they do not want to go it alone.) I pay them $60 per hour as a wage and I keep the other $40 per hour to cover the overhead of the business. After paying their wages, I collect $1,600 per employee per week or a total of $6,400 each week. Because I have to manage these four individuals, I can only bill out my time for 30 hours per week and collect $3,000 for my time. Adding this to the $6,400, I collect $9,400 each week for myself and to run the business. This allows me to pay the bills for overhead and if I have a slower week, it will not affect me as badly. On a monthly basis I am collecting just over $37,000 in revenue, which does not include the wages paid to each worker.

This is how the "multiplier effect" works. You find others to work for you and use part of their earnings to support the business.

In the MERI example in this book, the owner had several different workers with their own customer routes and generated business. The owner did not have to go out and fix machines personally, but spent time marketing, managing customers and running the business.

This concept is how you turn a business from a "mom and pop" outfit to a real sustainable business. Not all people are cut out to do this. Many do not want the headaches that go along with managing employees.

ABOUT THE AUTHOR

Randal Roberts

When our children (4 of them) married and left home, I needed something to do other than watch television. I was not a very good student in school, especially in English class, but for some reason, I have wanted to author a book. I do not know why.

I do have a lot of ideas, I am sure some better than others, but some of the things I have experienced have added to my understanding of buying, running and selling a business. So, I decided to write this book.

As a commercial banker, I have looked at over 4,000 different companies' financial information and have seen some very good and some not so good businesses. Some very large and some very small, in a broad range of industries. It really has been interesting seeing how different businesses are run and how some business seem to run the owners.

I hope my life experiences will help you secure your dream and move it along in the right direction.

Again, Good Luck!